D0153472

Religious Charter Schools

Legalities and Practicalities

A volume in
New Developments in the Politics of Education

Series Editor:
Bruce S. Cooper
Fordham University

New Developments in the Politics of Education

Bruce S. Cooper, Series Editor

Religious Charter Schools: Legalities and Practicalites (2007)
by Lawrence D. Weinberg

Religious Charter Schools

Legalities and Practicalities

by

Lawrence D. Weinberg

Information Age Publishing, Inc.
Charlotte, North Carolina • www.infoagepub.com

Library of Congress Cataloging-in-Publication Data

Weinberg, Lawrence D.
 Religious charter schools : legalities and practicalities / by Lawrence D. Weinberg.
    p. cm. -- (New developments in the politics of education)
 Includes bibliographical references.
 ISBN-13: 978-1-59311-758-0 (pbk.)
 ISBN-13: 978-1-59311-759-7 (hardcover)
 1. Religion in the public schools--Law and legislation--United States. 2. Charter schools--Law
and legislation--United States. 3. Church schools--Law and legislation--United States. I. Title.
 KF4162.W45 2007
 344.73'0796--dc22

                                                            2007016814

ISBN 13: 978-1-59311-758-0 (pbk.)
ISBN 13: 978-1-59311-759-7 (hardcover)
ISBN 10: 1-59311-758-2 (pbk.)
             1-59311-759-0 (hardcover)

Copyright © 2007 IAP–Information Age Publishing, Inc.

All rights reserved. No part of this publication may be reproduced, stored in a
retrieval system, or transmitted, in any form or by any means, electronic, mechanical,
photocopying, microfilming, recording or otherwise, without written permission
from the publisher.

Printed in the United States of America

CONTENTS

ACKNOWLEDGMENTS

The first thanks must go to Professor Charles L. Glenn, Jr. Dr. Glenn always encouraged me to finish this project and helped me create the theme of the book. I would also like to thank Professors David M. Steiner and Kenneth W. Simons, Esq. for their insightful comments.

I would also like to give special thanks to Professor Bruce S. Cooper of Fordham University, who not only helped me organize my thoughts but also provided me with encouragement and enthusiasm for this project and has graciously written a foreword. Additionally, I want to thank Professors Alan K. Gaynor and Vivian R. Johnson.

Lastly, I would like to dedicate this book to my father, Brian Weinberg (1945-1998), who finally now has a "doctor in the family."

ABSTRACT

This book explores the constitutionality of religion-based charter schools. The method of analysis uses hypothetical charter schools to answer legal questions. The answers are grounded in law using the latest precedent.

The background material before examining charters sets forth both the legal and policy contexts of religious charters schools. The legal context includes a detailed analysis of the Establishment Clause of the U.S. Constitution focusing on the most recent Supreme Court cases on that topic. The policy analysis examines the normative and structural dimensions of charter schools, which are then compared with voucher programs. The historical, political and educational contexts of charter programs are also examined.

Three hypothetical situations examine a total of 18 legal questions:

1. Can coreligionists form a charter school?
2. Can morality-based general propositions of good be taught in a charter school?
3. Can a charter school teach values espoused by coreligionists?
4. Can a charter school teach a course in the relationship between religion and morality?
5. Can a charter school have religious criteria for staff?
6. Can a charter school limit a teacher's right to express different worldviews?
7. Can a charter school offer optional prayer?

8.   Can a charter school form for the purpose of allowing students' ease of access to religious education?

9.   Can a charter school form to provide students, who would otherwise attend faith-based schools, with a free, secular public education?

10. Can clergy sit on the board of a charter school?

11. Can a charter school share facilities with a religious school?

12. Can a religious organization operate a charter school?

13. Can a charter school have religious criteria for admission?

14. To what extent can a religion class be taught in a charter school?

15.   Can a charter school require religious instruction?

16. Can a charter school require religious exercises or worship?

17. Can a charter school identify with a denomination?

18. Can states exclude religion-based charter schools from forming?

Each question is analyzed from a legal perspective.

The book concludes that charter schools present an opportunity for parents and communities to form charter schools that will accommodate their beliefs; however, the constitution does not allow them to form schools that endorse their beliefs.

FOREWORD

Bruce S. Cooper

Charter schools are quite the rage, with about 4,000 such schools now open, enrolling 1.1 million children in the United States—and more students participating in more charter schools every year. These schools obviously fulfill a real need in American society, giving local individuals, communities, and associations a chance to create their own schools, and to have tax dollars pay for the basic costs. It is a near perfect blend of *public* policy, funding, and responsibility mixed with *private* interests, choice, and needs. Go charters!

However, the one major unanswered, unresolved question since the charter school movement began in 1991 in Minnesota has been: *What about opening and supporting **religious** charter schools, initiated by Christian, Jewish, and Muslim groups?* In effect, are they legal—or how might they be legalized? This vital, excellent book by Lawrence Weinberg, *Religious Charter Schools: Legalities and Practicalities*, hits the mark. It discusses the complexities of legalizing charter schools with a religious, social, and cultural mission, tracing the legal arguments and court decisions back to the very roots of private education in the United States.

Starting in 1925, after the state of Oregon had passed a law requiring all students of school age to attend only a *public school* in their community, the issue came to court in *Pierce v. Society of Sisters*. The U.S. Supreme Court ruled that outlawing private, religious schools was unconstitutional, a violation of the First Amendment rights to free religious practices. But the court recognized that the right to *attend* private/religious schools was different from legalizing the *public funding* of religious schools. By 1965, over 12% of American children attended a private K-12 school, 80% of which were run by the Catholic Church. But all religious schools were privately financed by tuition and fees, donations, fund-raising (such as raffles, Christmas card sales, and bingo), and endowments.

Thus, the public funding of religious schools was still not allowed, although the major federal school legislation, the Elementary and Secondary Education Act (ESEA) of 1965—passed during the liberal Democratic coalition of the New Frontier under President Lyndon B. Johnson—did allow public school teachers and resources to service impoverished children attending their local private-religious schools. For without support of the U.S. Conference of Catholic Bishops, President Johnson might never have built the Democratic coalition he needed to get ESEA passed in the first place.

So, helping children in religious schools was not unknown or forbidden by law and policy; rather the courts had ruled continuously that the church-state separation meant no direct public dollars could pay for religious education, at least at the K-12 level. (The nation had always allowed military chaplains to offer religion services to soldiers; and college funding for religion classes under the GI Bill and Pell Grants as part of the university curriculum were not against the law.)

In this important book, Weinberg explains the major legal issues around public funding of religious charter schools. It is not legal, he shows, for public tax dollars to support any particular religious ideology, activity or program. In effect, public tax money cannot be used to endorse a belief system or religion. Hence, salaries for elementary and secondary school teachers of Bible, Koran, or catechism could not be paid from the public purse, if these teachers were endorsing these religious beliefs.

But what happened when a religious association, such as a Muslim group in Minneapolis, Minnesota, opened a school that was supportive of, and sensitive to the culture of Islam (its values, beliefs, and leaders) without being a Muslim religious charter school? How did this school, called the Tarek ibn Ziyad Academy, walk the "fine line" between serving a public purpose (educating children in a sensitive, culturally-specific, value-oriented program) while not being an Islamic religious school?

The Academy asks these questions of its families:

> Are you looking for a comprehensive/balanced education? A rigorous Arabic language program? An environment that fosters your cultural values and heritage? The Tarek ibn Ziyad Academy provides students with a learning environment that recognizes and appreciates the traditions, histories, civilizations and accomplishments of Africa, Asia, and the Middle East... It seeks to nurture the innate human values of brotherhood, equality, justice, compassion, and peace. Tarek Academy offers tuition-free education to all students upon admission.

This book explains the legal lenses starting with the separation of church and state, that established the principle that public funds could not be expended to support religious activity. First, in 1925, the *Pierce* decision protected the rights of private and religious schools to exist. And recently, in 2002, the Supreme Court decision in *Zelman v. Simmons-Harris* legalized the use of public vouchers (grants) to pay students' tuition at religious K-12 schools in Cleveland, Ohio, where this case originated, as long as the *family* was the determinant of where the child attended school. The money followed the child, and reflected family choice and values—and was not a government payment to religious schools.

Now the stage is set for a range of religious/cultural charter schools, paid for by the government (usually the state), as long as these schools follow the lead of Weinberg in this book. Charter schools have never been a unitary concept. Some states support them, while others do not. At present 40 of the 50 states, plus the District of Columbia, have charter school laws, each a little different, creating a whole complex national system of new schools in the United States.

New York State, for example, has a law that provides for the Board of Regents and the State University of New York to each charter up to 100 schools. Meanwhile, the city of New York also can charter schools within its boundaries, mainly schools with special themes or missions that fill a need in the system. Also, some systems are taking so-called "failing schools," under No Child Left Behind (those not making Adequate Yearly Progress, AYP), closing the school, and reopening it as a new, hopefully improved, local charter school. The "conversion charters" start often in the same building, with a new mission, theme, and staff—new wine in an old bottle.

And in the case of groups like the Edison Schools Project, a private for-profit corporation, they will be invited by the district to run existing schools or assume management of failing public schools and turn them into a charters. Charter schools thus come in many sizes and shapes—all having the interesting blend of private choice and leadership, supported and fostered with public funding! So why not also have religious groups starting charter schools, benefiting from the some $8,000 per student tuition payment, and thus creating a whole new species of schools?

We see this happening already in Minnesota and presumably soon in other localities. Religious groups can take the following steps to create legal charter schools:

- Create a foundation to manage the funding of the school building and to help raise money for the program.
- Write a charter school application under state law that specifies that the new charter school will be culturally sensitive to the religious groups being served, but not endorsing the tenets of the faith.
- State a mission that has specific educational and pedagogical objectives totally unrelated to the religious and cultural purposes but parallel to the faith.

- Design a curriculum that meets both purposes: that is, the religious/cultural sensitive program and the educational purposes.
- Focus recruitment on the particular religious group, while being open to admitting members of other faiths.

Religious Charter Schools: Legalities and Practicalities is perfectly timed. Charter schools have caught on. Religious charter schools have been attempted, and appear to be legal and workable. More will come, as other faiths see an opportunity to open schools with a clear cultural and ethical mission, a general pedagogy, and an attraction to members of their religious group.

So, everyone will want to read this book: academics and particularly professors of law and public policy will pour over the ideas and arguments. Religious group leaders will want to be sure to understand and possibly use the charter school laws to open their own schools. Parents will look to see what is happening that might affect their children.

The book introduces the concepts, giving a full legal analysis of the court cases, such as *Zelman* on vouchers; *Rosenberger v. University of Virginia* on determining that the public university was required to fund a Christian publication because it supported other student publications. In *Santa-Fe v. Doe*, the court held that a public school could not have students vote as to whether the school would hold prayer at school events; but individual students groups could study Bible or hold prayer for themselves. In *Mitchell v. Helms* the Supreme Court determined that secular Title 1 aid could go to religious schools since its purpose was to improve academic achievement, not to press a religious conversion.

In the large chapter 4, the Weinberg book answers real and practical questions that emerge when parents, teachers, administrators, and policymakers consider religion in charter school policies, such as: (1) Can a charter school require religious instruction? *No!* (2) Can clergy sit on the board of a charter school? *Yes!* (3) Can charter schools have religious criteria for hiring staff? *No!* (4) Can charter schools offer a place and time for students to pray? *Yes!* But (5), on the other hand, can charter schools *require* students to pray? *No!*

So for theorists, and legal eagles, this book treats in a scholarly manner the nature of the law and policies affecting charter schools. For practitioners and consumers of education, this book gives good advice for preventing some practices while rationalizing others. So can we imagine, having read this book, moving into another phase of American public and private education, one responding to the faith of the nation while respecting other beliefs?

These and other cases give a careful, comprehensive overview of the law, bringing the decisions to bear on the charter school issue. It is clearly not legal for state money, under charter legislation, to be allocated to operate and support a Catholic school. But, a Catholic association could create a St. Thomas Aquinas High School, where children learn the values and teachings of St. Thomas, but the teachings are cast in a cultural-academic setting, not as a Catholic, parochial school. Just as the Tarek Academy expresses its mission in Arabic (on its letterhead) and professes to expose students to the beliefs of this Islamic military leader and governor who lived over 1,300 years ago, the St. Thomas Academy, or one named after Rabbi Hillel for the Jews, could be formed to teach the ethics and history of the faith, but not to practice religion.

While it is a fine line, it is being drawn in the sand, and Weinberg is there, to help us understand what a religious charter school can do, and should not do. He is clear, rational, practical, and theoretical—all needed to understand and act upon the major American issue of religious charter schools: their possibilities, their limitations, and their future. Remember: accommodate, but do not endorse. Never forget that America is a religious society with an agnostic public school system.

Might we imagine a different school system, one where all schools are in some sense charters, fully funded by public taxes, available to all children based on parental choice, and as diverse as our society really is? Charter schools could offer us that chance, as Weinberg shows, to have a diverse, religious society, that respects cultures and beliefs, and offers families critical choices for their children's education.

It is coming, as big school systems break into school-by-school approaches; as vouchers are available and charter schools grow; and as the likelihood of religious charter schools increases. We know now that legal religious charters practice and respect the language, culture and religion of their sponsors—while not crossing the line and becoming a religious school. We are on the cusp of a revolution, and Lawrence Weinberg, in *Religious Charter Schools: Legalities & Practicalities*, is preparing us for the new world of U.S. education!

Bruce S. Cooper,
175 Riverside Drive, Apt. 2F
New York, NY 10024
TEL: 212 875-9371
Email: bruce.cooper@mac.com

Bruce S. Cooper, PhD, *is a professor at Fordham University Graduate School of Education, and editor the Private School MONITOR, a publication of the scholars' group, of the American Educational Research Association.*

PROLOGUE

INTRODUCTION

What would be a perfect formula for organizing a school with public, private, and religious qualities in the United States at this time? What if the school received tax dollars (e.g., $9,000 per pupil) under a program as a state charter school? What if the school were privately organized and managed, making it more responsive to parents and their needs? And what if the mission of the school were cultural, related to a religious group, so students were given a values-based, spiritual experience?

This mix describes a type of school in the United States that could be called a religiously-related charter school. Until now, this idea sounded interesting—particularly since the *Zelman* case (*Zelman v. Simmons-Harris*, 2002) legalized many voucher programs for religious schools—but had eluded the United States. The time is right, even ripe, to analyze the legality of religious charter schools—and see how they might work or not.

This book discusses the legality of religion-based charter schools. A charter school, like any state funded school, cannot endorse religion; the law is quite clear about that. However, a charter school, like any public school, can accommodate students' religions; the law is clear about that too. Charter schools are better able than public schools to accommodate their students' religious beliefs because they are smaller and are often created to serve a particular student population. A charter school can also endorse a culture.

No, the notion of religious charter schools is no oxymoron. Many such school are already operating in Minnesota—for example, The Tarek ibn Ziyad Academy—a charter school, located in Inver Grove Heights, Minnesota, that targets children of African, Asian, and Middle Eastern origin.

But have little doubt that this school is Islamic, or at least rests on Muslim culture and values: the school is named after a an Islamic leader of 1,300 years ago and has Arabic on its publicity offers an Arab language program. And other religiously-related charter schools exist too.

FEATURES OF A CONSTITUTIONAL CHARTER SCHOOL

What separates a constitutional school that accommodates religion and an unconstitutional school that endorses religion?

First, the constitutional school is likely to be run by separate nondenominational foundation. The foundation that owns the building and operates the school will be a freestanding entity whose only mission is to operate the school. The charity may have similar (or even the same) donors and board members as community religious organizations, but it will be a separate unit. This is not always necessary. For example, Augsburg College, a Lutheran University, sponsors the El Colegio Charter School in Minneapolis, Minnesota. However, the school does not appear to be in any way Lutheran.

Second, the primary mission of the school will be couched in general pedagogical terms. For example, the Tarek Academy's mission is to help children understand their stewardship role in the world, embedding in them a sense of "care, responsibility, love, leadership, civic participation, citizenship, tolerance and cooperation." These are all general pedagogical terms and could be found in almost any school.

Third, the school's religious elements are likely to be couched in cultural terms. For example, the Tarek Academy is named for Tarek ibn Ziyad a historically important Muslim leader. But the school's mission statement focuses on his role as "activist, leader, explorer, teacher, administrator and peacemaker." The school focuses on his nonreligious activities. But the subtext is clear. Tarek ibn Ziyad was the Muslim military leader who conquered the Iberian Peninsula and ruled it as its governor for the Muslim Caliphate.

Similarly, the Oh Day Aki (Heart of the Earth) Charter School of Minnesota's mission is to

> provide culturally-based education that is respectful to individual learning styles and interests and to support family and community participation in each student's education, resulting in the strengthening of American Indian culture while preparing students for higher education and self-sufficiency.

Here we see principals two and three. The school's mission addresses general values: individual learning styles and family and community participation. But an integral part of the mission is to teach American Indian culture. Culture and religion are often necessarily intertwined. Just as the Saturday sabbath and all its rituals are both part of the Jewish culture and religion one cannot separate many aspects American Indian culture and religion.

Other cultures are easier to distinguish from their religions. The Academia Cesar Chavez is dedicated to a community-based, holistic approach to education through quality academics by utilizing Latino culture in an environment of family and community; 237 of the school's 246 students are Hispanic. A school with a mission that explicitly references Latino culture and has an overwhelmingly Hispanic student population is going to be more likely to accommodate the needs of Catholic students than a school with a different mission. There is nothing unconstitutional about endorsing a culture or accommodating religion.

What is important is that the constitutional school articulates its mission in cultural terms rather than religious language. The accommodation of students' religious beliefs is a matter for the day-to-day operation of the school, not the mission statement.

Fourth, the school will not have religious requirements. The school will not require prayer. A school may adjust its schedule to take into account the religious needs of its Muslim or Jewish or Catholic majority students. The school may set aside time in its schedule for prayer. The school may set aside a room for prayer. But the school will not provide the books used by the students to pray and certainly won't require them to pray. For example, the Web site for the Adam Abdulle Academy (2007), another Minnesota charter school that caters to an immigrant population, explicitly states, "Academy is a public charter school and is not affiliated with any religion. The Academy is nonsectarian with regard to program, admission, employment, and curriculum."

Fifth, the school cannot require that students profess any particular faith. Constitutional schools won't require students to be Muslim or Jewish or Catholic. However, a school may offer courses that will be of interest to a particular faith. For example, the Tarek Academy offers a rigorous Arabic language program. The school may target students who are Muslim or Jewish or Catholic to recruit them; however, this must be done in a very careful fashion.

Six, the school will have features that are wholly unrelated to religion. For example, the Tarek Academy utilizes the Saxon Math and Scott Foresman Reading social studies and science books. The Adam Abdulle Academy incorporates mentorships and daily reading and writing into its school program.

WHY RELIGION-BASED CHARTER SCHOOLS ARE FORMING

The United States is a diverse and religious country. According to a 2003 Harris poll, 79% of Americans believe in god and 55% of Americans attend a church multiple times per year. A 2006 Gallup Poll found that 73% of Americans are convinced God exists, an additional 14% believe god probably exists and have a little doubt. Ninety percent of children in private schools attend religious schools. Historically education and religion were intimately connected. Although we currently view public education as necessarily nonreligious, the nineteenth-century vision of the common school was in many ways Protestant.

Religion still plays a remarkable role in American life. Although structured prayer is no longer permitted in public schools, prayer can be found in state legislatures throughout the country and opens Congress. Furthermore, even though the Constitution prohibits prayer at school functions, it can be found at public school activities in small districts where no parents complain.

Although we view the separation between church and state as a wall, the late Chief Justice Burger referred to it as a "blurred, indistinct, and variable barrier" (*Lemon v. Kurtzman*, 1971, 403 U.S. 602, 614). The requirements of the separation between church and state are particularly complicated when one looks at charter schools. As a general matter, the state may fund secular functions of religious schools when it similarly funds those functions at public schools. For example, the state may pay for secular library and curriculum materials and then loan those materials to private religious schools (*Mitchell v. Helms*, 2000). The state may provide a sign language interpreter to a deaf child attending a parochial school (*Zobrest v. Catalina Foothills Sch. Dist.*, 1993). The state, however, may not itself engage in religious activities in public school. Charter schools are privately managed but publicly funded, which adds an additional level of analysis.

FOCUS OF THE BOOK

This book explains everything you need to know to understand the theoretical and practical implications of religion-based charter schools. Chapter one provides an overview and an explanation of the purposes of the book. After reading this book you will understand what a charter school is where it came from and how it operates. Charter schools are founded and supported privately. Charter schools build on the interests of the community and family. The original idea was that charter schools would compete with public schools and inspire them to be better. Help the charter school to improve the quality of public schools.

The book then discusses the First Amendment and the notions of the separation between church and state developed over 200 years. Chapter two examines the legal background, in particular the requirements of the Establishment Clause, explaining the requirement that the government act neutrally with respect to religion. The chapter explains the nonfunding principle the Supreme Court has applied to religious education for the past 60 years. The Constitution requires that any state act must have a secular purpose, cannot have the primary effect of advancing or inhibiting religion, and cannot create an excessive entanglement between church and state (*Lemon v. Kurtzman*, 1971). The chapter then describes the current trends in the Supreme Court, closely examining its most recent cases.

Chapter three provides the reader with the historical and theoretical background to understand charter schools as a method of school choice. The principle that epitomizes the expectation of all charter schools is "accountability for autonomy" ("Charter School," 1998). Accountability is nearly always defined in terms of student achievement. Autonomy occurs through reducing state and district interference.

Although choice comes in many forms (e.g., intradistrict choice, magnet schools), the primary current forms of choice under policy discussion are charters and vouchers. The difference between charter and voucher systems is in the manner that the state implements a choice system. Vouchers realize choice by giving parents money (in the form of a voucher) to choose among private and out-of-district schools. Charters implement choice by creating free schools to which parents can send their children. Although support for vouchers has grown slowly, public support for school choice has increased.

This book next addresses the practical dos and don'ts of religious charter schools. Chapter four is a detailed examination of the issues facing religion-based charter schools. That chapter examines three hypothetical charter schools and the legal questions those schools pose. The chapter answers eighteen separate legal questions facing those who want to create a charter school.

The questions posited by the hypothetical schools focus on practical aspects of founding and operating a charter school while also illustrating how charter schools shift the balance of power between the state and parents. The answers to these questions will illustrate that charter schools cannot be considered in terms of a religious organization's access to a state facility nor as a mere funding program. The answers also demonstrate that parents can create charter schools that accommodate their religious beliefs, but not such schools that endorse their religion.

The final chapter the book looks to the future as more religion-based charter schools form. Chapter five also reexamines the legal and other contexts of charter schools, with the perspective gained by examining the hypothetical situations. The chapter also summarizes all the answers to the questions found in chapter four. The basic findings are that a charter school can form to accommodate parents' religious beliefs; however, a charter school cannot endorse parents' religious beliefs.

THIS BOOK'S FOUR AUDIENCES

This book is written for four types of readers: (1) professors and policymakers interested in law and education, (2) parents thinking about starting a charter school; (3) religious community leaders and educators, and (4) school leaders, such as principals or superintendents.

Professors and policymakers interested in law and education do not have a source that examines both the theoretical and legal background necessary to examine religious charter schools.

This book answers the questions on the minds of religious community leaders and religious educators thinking about starting a charter school. This book also answers the questions on the minds of parents thinking about sending their children to a religious charter school. Those questions include: Can clergy sit on the board of a charter school? Can a charter school offer optional prayer? Can a charter school form for the purpose of allowing students ease of access to religious education? Can a charter school have religious criteria for staff? Can states exclude religion-based charter schools from forming? Can a religious organization operate a charter school? Can a charter school identify with a denomination?

School leaders principals, superintendents will read this book not because they want to start a charter school, but because they want to address the needs of their religious populations without endorsing religion. For example, principals want to know to what extent student initiated prayer is permitted in a public school.

WHY THIS BOOK IS UNIQUE

This book is unique because it is both theoretical and practical. It answers the questions posed by policymakers, the why's. It also answers the questions asked by parents and educators who want practical answers, the what's and the how's.

Another difference between this book and what previously has been written about charter schools is that this book does not make the assumptions that drive other books to foregone conclusions. Most authors either assume from the beginning of their analysis that religious charter schools are constitutional or that religious charters are not constitutional. They do not look at the reality, which is that some religious activities by charter schools are constitutional and others are not. A religious charter school can take many forms. This book tries to answer the questions related to which of those forms are allowed by law.

Consequently, no one is going to be happy with this book. It does not argue for all religious charters or argue for a strong wall of separation. I would expect criticism from the "right" and the "left." But it is the first book that looks at religious charter schools in a balanced, logical, and historical way.

The line drawn by this book, that charter schools may accommodate religious belief, but not endorse religious beliefs may not please anyone. But it strictly follows the precedents set by the U.S. Supreme Court and representative other courts around the country. Also, this line is representative of how Americans live their religious lives. We believe. We practice. But in the end, we try not to impose our religious beliefs on others.

CHAPTER 1

CAN RELIGIOUS CHARTER SCHOOLS BE CONSTITUTIONAL?

INTRODUCTION

This book analyzes of whether a religion-based charter school could legally and constitutionally form. This is not a simple question and it does not yield a simple answer. A religion-based charter school could take many forms: some would be constitutionally permitted, while others would violate the separation between church and state.

Charter schools radically affect the balance between the state and the citizen by offering parents the opportunity to create public schools that are responsive to their needs. With regard to parents' religious beliefs, charter schools allow parents to create public schools that accommodate their religious beliefs and needs. The Supreme Court has "long recognized that the government may (and sometimes must) accommodate religious practices and that it may do so without violating the Establishment Clause" (*Hobbie v. Unemployment Appeals Comm'n of Fla.*, 1987, 480 U.S. 136, 144-45).

Public schools accommodate religious beliefs by giving consideration to those religious beliefs and providing something that is beneficial to adherents of those beliefs, without necessarily adapting the entire school

Religious Charter Schools: Legalities and Practicalites, pp. 1–15
Copyright © 2007 by Information Age Publishing
All rights of reproduction in any form reserved.

program to those beliefs. However, charter schools may not endorse parents' religious beliefs. Charter schools are not merely a funding program; nor do they merely provide access to public facilities. Charter school legislation enables parents to create public schools; as public schools, they are bound by the same legal constraints as any public school.

The power to create schools that accommodate their religious beliefs can be very important to many of the parents who are most disaffected with public schools. For example, *Mozert v. Hawkins*, a 1987 Court of Appeals case that will be discussed in depth later in this chapter, involved very religious parents who sued their children's school district because they were unhappy with the school readers. Charter schools present such parents with the opportunity to create a free public school that, while it does not teach their religious beliefs, also does not teach lessons that they find religiously objectionable. This may mean as much (or more) to some religious parents as the ability to create a denominational school.

States have thus far defined charter schools as public schools making them state actors bound by the U.S. Constitution; consequently, whether a religion-based charter school can operate is much more than a mere funding issue. It is unclear whether a state could define charter schools as nonstate actors. On the other hand a state cannot close its school system to get around constitutional requirements (*Griffin v. County Sch. Bd of Prince Edward County*, 1964).

Charter schools represent a form of public education controlled by parents and small constituencies rather than by a state or a local district. Consequently, the charter form of school organization shifts the balance of control toward the parent and away from the state. The basic principle behind the charter movement is autonomy for accountability ("Charter Schools," 1998). One starting definition is that a charter school is an "independent public school of choice, freed from the rules but accountable for results" (Finn, Manno, & Vanourek, 2000, p. 14). Charter schools have more freedom than traditional public schools, but they are more directly accountable for results since their charters may be revoked if they do not meet performance goals. In return for autonomy, a school's charter stipulates academic, organizational, and/or financial standards to which the charter school will be accountable. A group applies for a charter from the state to operate a school and agrees to meet certain criteria defined by that charter. These criteria vary from state to state and from charter to charter.

America's constitutional democracy is based on balancing the conflicting powers, rights, and needs of the state and the individual. Charter schools can be viewed as a means of adjusting this balance. The state allows individuals to form and operate public schools; in return, the individuals agree to meet specific criteria defined by the state.

The U.S. Constitution does not mandate charter schools, but the Constitution does protect parents who disagree with the state's educational aims. The Constitution guarantees the right to use private education, prohibits the state from requiring students to commit acts that violate their religious beliefs, prevents compulsory education that would endanger an established religious community's way of life, and bans the state from sponsoring prayer at graduations (*Pierce v. Society of Sisters*, 1925; *Santa Fe v. Doe*, 2000; *West Virginia v. Barnette*, 1943; *Wisconsin v. Yoder*, 1972).

Charter schools also offer parents who are uncomfortable with the culture or curriculum of most public schools, whether for religious or secular reasons, the opportunity to provide their children with a free public education. Arons (1983) notes, "amidst [the] cultural conflict it is sometimes difficult for the outside observer to remain aware that members of dissenting communities are in pursuit of life goals and meaning that transcend state policy and mundane concerns" (p. 179). It is often easy for someone to say, "What's the big deal with a prayer at a football game?" or, "What's the big deal with reading a Harry Potter book?" Many parents, because of their religious or philosophical beliefs, care very deeply and very appropriately.

Conflicts involving education reverberate to the core of the supposed "culture wars." Education is important to the government, which needs education to perpetuate the democratic political system, and to individual families, who need education to perpetuate their values, culture, and religion. Public education has become one of the quintessential functions of the modern state. The Supreme Court in *Brown v. Board of Education of Topekas* said, "Today, education is perhaps the most important function of state and local governments" (1954, 347 U.S. 483, 493). The Supreme Court has declared that public schools "as instruments of the state, [may determine the] essential lessons of civil mature conduct" (*Bethel School District v. Fraser*, 1986, 478 U.S. 675, 683).

The Court, however, has also noted "the rights of parents to direct the religious upbringing of their children" (*Wisconsin v. Yoder*, 1972, 406 U.S. 205, 233). Thus, both the state and parents can point to the Constitution to validate their interests and rights with regard to education. Neither the parent nor the state can possess an absolute right to direct the education of a child. Charter schools are one means of achieving an appropriate balance between these two sets of interests and rights.

WHAT IS A RELIGION-BASED CHARTER SCHOOL?

Some authors argue that the Constitution permits charter schools to be religious. Those authors describe religious schools in general terms: "Let religious schools become part of the charter system so long as they're willing to abide by the results-based accountability arrangements that other charter schools must accept" (Finn, 2003). Consequently, those authors assume that a religious charter school can operate in the same manner as a private religious school. We will see, however, that this assumption is unwarranted. This book examines several forms of religion-based charter schools, including the indoctrinating school and a school formed for religious reasons, even if the school's program is itself secular.

Chapter four, which examines hypothetical charter schools, discusses three very different models of how a religion-based charter school would form and operate. Religious parents may choose to form a charter school for many diverse motivations and this work tries to examine a significant range of those reasons.

The application of *Zelman v. Simmons-Harris* (2002), the recent Supreme Court voucher decision, to charter schools, is often overstated, ignoring that charter schools are public schools and are state actors with very different constitutional requirements than private schools. Moreover, a religion-based charter school is not only a private faith-based school that is now formed under a charter rather than as a private school, but rather it is a school formed by parents who chartered it for religious reasons.

MOZERT V. HAWKINS, PARENTS' RIGHTS, AND THE STATE

A federal appellate court case, *Mozert v. Hawkins* (1987), illustrates the tensions between the state and parents regarding education. *Mozert* is not important because of its value as legal precedent, as an appellate division case it has considerably less value than a Supreme Court Decision. *Mozert*, however, is also an excellent springboard to discuss the question of whether religious charter schools are constitutional because it is very likely that the type of parents who sued in that case who would be drawn to charter schools. It is also an example of the discord that sometimes develops between the state and parents over how to direct a child's education.

In 1983, seven families sued the Hawkins County Board of Education arguing that forcing their elementary-school-aged children to read certain stories from the Holt, Rinehart, and Winston reading series ("Holt series") violated their right to freely exercise their religion. Although the school had initially created an alternative reading program for parents who found the reading objectionable, the school board eliminated that program in November of 1983; this incited the parents to sue.

One parent, for example, Vicki Frost, who described herself as a "born again Christian" had a religious objection to any teaching about mental telepathy, references to secular humanism, evolution, futuristic supernaturalism, pacifism, magic, and false views of death. At trial, Mrs. Frost testified that an occasional reference to the subjects would be acceptable, but that she objected to the repeated references to these subjects, saying that she objected to the reading series as a whole. Mrs. Frost, however, also testified that there was "no way" certain themes could be presented without violating her religious beliefs.

The Federal Court of Appeals for the Sixth Circuit held that religious parents do not have the constitutional right to prevent their children from learning about things that violate their religious beliefs. Although parents have the right to prevent their publicly-schooled children from committing acts, or making affirmations, against their religious beliefs (*West Virginia v. Barnette*, 1943), parents do not have the right to prevent their children from being exposed to ideas that run contrary to those beliefs. The Court also noted the school district's interest in a uniform curriculum. Consequently, Mrs. Frost and other parents could not force their school district to exempt their children from reading material they found objectionable for religious reasons. Nor could parents force the district to pay tuition for their children to attend an alternative school.

Mozert v. Hawkins illustrates the potential for conflict between parents and schools over the education of children, particularly when religious issues are present. The school has an interest in a uniform curriculum, while the parent has an interest in protecting her child from exposure to religiously offensive ideas, especially when those ideas are presented with the authority of the state as part of the required curriculum of a public school. The school and parent differ as to what the child should and should not learn.

Mozert v. Hawkins is a starting point for a discussion about religion-based charter schools because it is parents who are disaffected with the public school system who are the most likely to form a religion-based charter school. In fact, most of the parents who sued in *Mozert* home-schooled their children, sent their children to private religious schools, or transferred them to other school districts when the school district eliminated the reading alternatives to the Holt series. In 1983, forming a charter school was not then an option for them.

The prospect of such a school begs the question: what would be the constitutional implications if Mrs. Frost and like-minded parents proposed to establish a state-funded charter school where the curriculum did not contain those stories or other materials that they found objectionable? Should such a charter school be considered religious? Would it be found constitutional? Would the religious motivations of the parents in forming such a charter school make it unconstitutional? Conversely, would a school formed for secular reasons, but which taught religious content, be constitutional? There are many different types of potential "religious" charter schools. Some would be constitutional and others not. In fact, religious charter schools of some fashion are likely inevitable and in some forms already exist.

Most parents, unlike the Frosts, do not sue their school district; many more simply withdraw their children. Even in our litigation-ready society, it takes a profound dissatisfaction with a curriculum or decision before parents opt to sue or to leave the public school system. In theory, the rights of many or most parents and the state should not conflict. Such is the nature of democracy; the laws passed by the legislature elected by the majority should suit the majority's needs. Whether this works in practice with respect to a school system is debatable. However, it is not the majority of parents who form charter schools. It is a minority of parents who are troubled by their local school districts, for reasons relating to academics, religion, safety, or other factors, who form charter schools.

The Constitution protects the rights of political, racial, and religious minorities. Minority rights are never absolute, just as the state's powers are never absolute. For example, even when the state makes a distinction among its citizens on the basis of race, the state must have a compelling interest and the legislation must be narrowly tailored to meet that interest (e.g., *Brown v. Board of Education*, 1954). This standard, called "strict scrutiny," is the highest standard that courts use to examine legislation. The strict scrutiny standard also applies when the state tries to censor the expression of its citizens. The state must have a compelling reason for the censorship and that censorship must be narrowly tailored to the reason.

The federal Constitution does not protect the parental right to educate children as powerfully as it protects the right of persons not to be distinguished on the basis of race or the right not to be censored. It is, however, important to bear in mind that even those rights (i.e., preventing discrimination and censorship) that are most important to the individual in our democratic constitutional system are not absolute. Conversely, it is equally important to bear in mind that when the state is exercising its rights, or rather its authority over the populace, that authority is never absolute. Even the state's ability to regulate members of the military, while it is given great deference by the courts, is not absolute. Although the state has greater authority to regulate military personnel than it does the general populace, the rights guaranteed soldiers by the First Amendment are not nullified through their enlistment (*Goldman v. Weinberger*, 1986).

Often, when the state exercises its power, the federal Constitution's limitation is merely that the state must act rationally. Even such a minor limitation is notable because the provisions of the Constitution nearly always balance between the rights and duties of the state and the individual. This balance is particularly important in education. Therefore, the lesson of

Mozert v. Hawkins, is not that parents have no rights when it comes to educating their children. Nor is the lesson that the state power to regulate the curriculum trumps the parental right to direct the education of her children. The Frosts still have rights. The state cannot force their children to commit an act or make an affirmation that violates their religious beliefs.

The state cannot force the Frosts to send their children to public school. If parents had no rights vis-à-vis education, that would give the state far too much power in a democracy. The lesson of *Mozert* is that the state can require the Frosts to choose between a free public education and selecting what lessons their children will learn and what their children will read. Charter schools, however, open the possibility of the Frosts not having to make that choice. Therefore, charter schools directly affect the balance of individual rights and the state's authority in favor of parents.

INEVITABILITY OF RELIGION-BASED CHARTER SCHOOLS

The number of charter schools in the United States is increasing. As of September 2006, 3,977 charter schools are operating in forty states and the District of Columbia (Center for Education Reform, 2006). The total enrollment exceeds one million students. States continue to enact charter legislation. Portland, Oregon even considered making the entire district subject to charters (Bierwirth, 1997). Charter schools are also expanding in Canada (Bossetti, 1998).

Although states generally currently exclude denominational schools from applying for charters, it is inevitable that religiously-motivated parents, like the Frosts, and groups will apply for charters to establish schools. Eventually, religiously oriented charter schools are likely to appear across the country. In fact, lawsuits have already been decided involving potentially religious charter schools. Parents unsuccessfully sued in Michigan to have the state deny charter status to a school, arguing that a charter school was religious (*Daugherty v. Vanguard Charter Academy*, 2000). Similarly, a reverend in Milwaukee unsuccessfully sued arguing that his school was denied charter school status on the basis of his religious beliefs (*Perry v. Milwaukee Public Schools*, 2001).

Religious charter schools are likely to form for three very different reasons. First, many parents have the desire for religion-based charter schools. Second, some states may possibly eliminate of the secular requirements in charter legislation. Third, recent Supreme Court decisions invite the argument that religious charter schools are constitutional.

The primary reason that religion-based charter schools are inevitable is that religious organizations and parents will try to circumvent state restrictions and form charter schools. Experience shows that those who start independent schools, and those who choose them, are more often than not motivated by religious considerations. Religious parents flock to alternative education because they "firmly believe they must raise their children to be good Jews or good Muslims, or good born-again Christians, and so on" (Sweet, 1997, p. 110). Evangelicals, for example, flocked to charter schools in Colorado (Morken & Formicola, 1999, p. 57). In fact, one of the reasons used by the Supreme Court when prohibiting state aid to private schools is that private schools are overwhelmingly parochial (*Lemon v. Kurtzman*, 1971).

Parental desire to form religion-based charter schools is illustrated by the response to the New York charter statute, which was passed in December 1998. The New York State charter school statute states,

> A charter school shall be non-sectarian in its programs, admission policies, employment practices, and all other operations.... A charter shall not be issued to any school that would be wholly or in part under the control or direction of any religious denomination, or in which any denominational tenet or doctrine would be taught. (N.Y. Educ. Law § 2854(2) (a) (2007)

Despite the obvious prohibition against operating a religiously-oriented charter school, leaders in various denominations began planning to open charter schools less than 2 months after the charter legislation passed. The most outspoken was Reverand Floyd Flake, a former congressman and the senior pastor at the Allen African Methodist Episcopal Church (Hartocollis, 1999). Similarly, lawyers for the Kiryas Joel Union Free School District, an all Satmar Hassidic school district and community involved in much litigation over the district's creation, investigated whether the district could use charter school legislation to provide public schooling for the district's handicapped children (Brodsky, 1999).

Minnesota requires that charter schools must be nonsectarian in their programs, admission policies, employment practices, and all other operations and prohibits charters affiliated with a nonpublic sectarian school or a religious institution (Minn. Stat. Ann. § 124D.10 subd. 8 (c) 2004). Nonetheless, the Tarek ibn Ziyad Academy in Minnesota rests on Muslim culture and values. Religious persons or organizations that apply for charters will invariably draft applications in religiously-neutral language to satisfy the New York, Minnesota, or other state statute.

Second, although state charter laws presently exclude religious charter schools, it is presumable that some states will in the future approve religious charter schools. When states began instituting vouchers they excluded religious schools from the programs. Some states, notably Wisconsin, Ohio, and Florida, now include religious schools in the voucher programs they run in school districts. The Wisconsin statute when originally enacted in 1993 required that private schools that participate in the program be "nonsectarian" (§119.23). The statute, however, was amended in 1995 to allow participation by religious schools (*Jackson v. Benson*, 1998). The Wisconsin State Supreme Court held that including religious schools was constitutional under the state and federal constitutions (*Id.*). The Supreme Court denied review. Both the U.S. and Ohio Supreme Courts have held constitutional including religious schools in the Cleveland voucher program (*Simmons-Harris v. Goff*, 1999; *Zelman v. Simmons-Harris*, 2002). These cases and others will be discussed more fully in chapter two.

Lastly, religious organizations could argue that recent Supreme Court precedent not only allows religious charters, but also requires that religious and nonreligious charters be funded in the same manner. *Rosenberger v. University of Virginia* (1995) held that the University of Virginia could not deny funding to a Christian student group's publication. The Supreme Court held that the Establishment Clause did not bar funding the group's publication because the funding statute was neutral. Moreover, the university could not deny funding because to deny a religious group funding for a newspaper would be unconstitutional viewpoint discrimination (censorship).

In 2001 the Supreme Court held that a New York school district could not ban parents from operating a religious after school club once it allowed secular groups to operate similar clubs (*Good News Club v. Milford Central School*, 2001). Lastly, advocates such as Chester Finn (2003), have argued that *Zelman v. Simmons-Harris* (2002), the Ohio voucher case that was decided by the Supreme Court, indicates that religion-based charter schools are constitutional. These cases and others will be discussed more fully in chapter two.

Although charter schools are not newspapers, they do espouse alternative viewpoints. One of the reasons for enacting charter school legislation has been so that charter schools could evolve and express distinctive character. Enacting charter school legislation creates, as Arons (1983) argues, "separation between school and state" (p. 189). Not funding religious charters could be viewed as discriminating against religious viewpoints. The state and education establishments consistently fight dissent (Arons, p. 191). Funding one, but not the other, could be perceived as unequal. There is a growing trend for groups with minority beliefs to turn to the courts (Glenn, 1988, p. 279). This argument will be discussed in more detail in later chapters.

The purpose of this book is not to state where the balance between parents and state should be, but rather to take those existing scales and apply them to the issue of religious charter schools. This book does not attempt to describe the goals or inner workings of charter schools, but rather uses the existing descriptions to examine the possibility of religious charters. Similarly, this work does not attempt to describe fully the constitutional requirement of the separation between church and state, but to use existing studies along with relevant case law, to address the specific issues that relate to religion-based charter schools.

This book examines religion-based charter schools for three reasons. First, such schools are on the horizon. For the reasons discussed above, it is most likely only a matter of time before religious charter schools are organized and already exist—though unacknowledged—in some form already. Second, religious charter schools are a novel policy issue. Charter schools question our fundamental understanding of what a public school is. Consequently, studies of larger policy issues in education will address the issue of charter schools in some form. Religious charter schools are also one of the most radical and interesting forms to examine. Third, the constitutionality of religious charter schools is a novel legal question. Although most current school choice litigation involves school vouchers, such litigation cannot settle the constitutionality of religion-based charter schools because charter programs are philosophically and legally different from voucher programs.

Accordingly, this analysis assumes the future growth of demand for and existence of religious charter schools. Just as voucher statutes initially precluded religious schools but now are beginning to include them, so also some state charter school statutes will probably come to include religious charter schools. Additionally, it is often religious parents who are most uncomfortable with public schools and are driven to opening private or alternative schools. Religiously-motivated parents almost certainly sit on current charter school boards and influence the development of those schools, as it would be unconstitutional to exclude religious parents from charter school boards (*McDaniel v. Paty*, 1978). Would a charter school entirely of such parents be unconstitutional? Would such a board make the charter school necessarily religious?

Clergy who are also community leaders, such as Floyd Flake, are already considering how to open charter schools. Would a charter school operated under the auspices of a church or minister be constitutional? What if the principal was ordained, but did not have a pulpit? May legislatures exclude religious groups from opening charter schools? Religion-based charter schools pose these and many other interesting questions. Lastly, recent Supreme Court cases indicate that the Court holds that religious groups cannot constitutionally be excluded from some state-funded programs. Are charter schools such a program?

OVERVIEW

This book examines whether and in what form religion-based charter schools are constitutional. Chapter two examines the issue within its legal context, looking generally at Establishment Clause law. Chapter three explores various threshold issues regarding charter schools. These include the normative and structural dimensions of charter schools, which the chapter compares with vouchers. Chapter three also looks at the historical, political, and educational contexts of charter schools. Chapter four utilizes three hypothetical schools to illustrate the various constitutional issues that may be present when a religious charter school forms. The three hypotheticals are as follows: (1) an ostensibly nonreligious, morally-based school founded by coreligionists; (2) a half-time secular school structured to allow children to attend religious training during part of the day; and (3) a charter school operated by a religious organization. Finally, the concluding chapter summarizes the previous findings and analyzes legal and policy issues left open or changed by the potential of religious charter schools.

Chapter two examines the legal background, in particular the requirements of the Establishment Clause. The separation between church and state is a complicated principle that has been described in elusive metaphorical terms by the Supreme Court (*Lemon v. Kurtzman*, 1971; *McCollum v. Board of Ed.*, 1948; *Tilton v. Richardson*, 1971). Moreover, the words "separation between church and state" are not even the words of the First Amendment, which prohibits "respecting an establishment of religion" and bans Congress (and the states through the Fourteenth Amendment) from "prohibiting the free exercise thereof." Moreover, scholars (and often Courts) have disagreed over the meaning of the religion clauses and even whether they apply to the states at all (compare Cord, 1982 with Pfeffer, 1967; compare Levy, 1994 with Berger, 1997).

Quite simply, the religion clauses require that the government act neutrally with respect to religion. Of course, neutrality is not always easily defined. The seminal establishment clause cases are *Everson v. Board of Education of Ewing Twp.* (1947) and *Lemon v. Kurtzman* (1971). The specific holdings of these two cases are not as important as the principles they describe. *Everson* was the case that applied the nonfunding principle (limiting state aid to religious institutions) to religious education and applied the Establishment Clause to the states. *Lemon* defined the three-prong test that courts used for the next thirty years to decide most Establishment Clause cases. The three prongs were that a statute must have a secular purpose, cannot have the primary effect that advances or inhibits religion, and cannot create an excessive entanglement between church and state. Courts used the *Lemon* test consistently until the Supreme Court in 1997 in *Agostini v. Felton* merged the entanglement prong with the effect prong and now look at entanglement as an aspect of effect rather than as a separate issue.

At the current time, the trend in the Supreme Court is toward allowing indirect aid to go to faith-based schools. Indirect aid has been found to be constitutional so long as the criteria for giving out the aid are religiously neutral (*Agostini v. Felton* 1997; *Mitchell v. Helms*, 2000; *Zelman v. Simmons-Harris*, 2002). Recent Supreme Court jurisprudence has also required that school districts allow religious organizations to have equal access to facilities and has prohibited schools denying organizations from using their facilities on the basis of their religious orientation (*Good News Club v. Milford Central School*, 2001; *Rosenberger v. University of Virginia*, 1995). An important feature of these cases is that access is required on the basis of the Free Speech Clause; the Establishment Clause merely *allows* access, but does not *demand* it. The final trend with regard to church and state in the Supreme Court is that it will generally not allow religious activities by the state. The state cannot endorse religion and cannot use the formality of a student election to insert prayer into a school-sponsored activity (*Santa Fe v. Doe*, 2000).

Although the most recent Supreme Court cases have held constitutional the state's funding of secular activities at religious schools, those cases do not mean that religion-based charters are constitutional. The aid cases have made a strong distinction between per-capita aid programs, which are unconstitutional, and true private choice programs, which the constitution allows (*Mitchell v. Helms*, 2000; *Zelman v. Simmons-Harris*, 2002). It is far from clear whether charters would fall under one category or the other, but it is likely that a charter school program would be considered a per-capita aid program. Per-capita aid is always unconstitutional when money goes to a religious school. It is also far from clear that the access cases decide the issue for religion-based charter schools. However, the access cases provide a very strong argument that charters cannot be excluded because their founders have a religious viewpoint. Lastly, because charter schools are public schools and likely state actors, they can not encourage student prayer, or other religious activities. These cases are discussed in much greater depth in chapter two.

Chapter three examines charter schools from a policy perspective. To understand charter schools it is necessary to be aware of their normative, structural, political, historical, and educational underpinnings. The normative principle that epitomizes the expectation of all charter schools is "accountability for autonomy" ("Charter School," 1998; Finn, Manno, & Vanourek, 2000, p. 14). Accountability is nearly always defined in terms of student achievement. Autonomy occurs through reducing state and district interference.

Charter schools are a relatively recent phenomenon, having started in Minnesota in 1991. Charter statutes vary widely in structure and practice from state to state. Charter schools form for various reasons that can be divided into four categories: (1) to implement innovative programs; (2) to educate more effectively or efficiently; (3) to provide choices; and (4) to inspire public schools to be better. Charter schools are different from public schools (depending on the state), in that they can be created by almost anyone, are exempt from most state and local regulations, are chosen by the families of children who attend, and may be closed if they do not achieve acceptable results (Finn, Manno, & Vanourek, 2000, pp. 14-15).

Charter schools are one form of school choice. The modern school choice movement can be traced to a 1955 essay by Milton Friedman (Viteritti, 1999, p. 2, citing Friedman, 1955). Although choice comes in many forms (e.g., intradistrict choice, magnet schools), the primary current forms of choice under policy discussion are charters and vouchers. Of course, school choice is always available if you have the wherewithal to move to another school district or can afford private school tuition (Wise, 1968). Support for vouchers has grown slowly and public support for school choice has increased over the past ten years (Fusarelli, 2003, p. 3; Viteritti, 1999, p. 5).

The difference between charter and voucher systems is in the manner that the state implements a choice system. Vouchers realize choice by giving parents money (in the form of a voucher) to choose among private and out-of-district, public schools. Charters implement choice by creating free schools to which parents can send their children. The legal distinction between these programs becomes clear reading Justice O'Connor's concurrence in *Mitchell v. Helms* in 2000. (The case is discussed in depth in chapter 2.)

Although the notion of public education has changed greatly in the past 150 years, the nineteenth century vision of public schooling as an instrument for social unity resonates today. Compulsory public education has come to mean not only that all citizens are educated, but that, for good or ill, they have nearly uniform educational experiences. The relationship between religion and education has also changed drastically in the past 150 years, when neutrality in education meant that only the great truths of Christianity were taught in public schools. The change in that relationship accelerated in the 1960s and the division between religion and public education continues today.

The strongest argument in favor of charter schools is that the public school should be the basic unit of management (Hill, Guthrie, & Pierce, 1997, pp. 8, 56–57). When schools are more concerned with fulfilling government mandates than community needs, parents feel disaffected by their complete removal from the decision-making process (pp. 31–32). Public schools have created this problem by growing as a monopoly, consequently eliminating reasons to function efficiently (Peterson, 1990).

Public education has become America's most common cultural experience and its biggest business (Arons, 1983, p. 88). Since the publication of *A Nation at Risk* in 1985, educational reformers have proposed various means of combating the "rising tide of mediocrity" (p. 5)The radical change proposed by charter schools has its roots in the problems caused by the uniformity of public schools (Sarason, 1998).

Chapter four is a detailed examination of the issues facing religion-based charter schools. That chapter examines three hypothetical charter schools and the legal questions those schools pose. The chapter is not meant to be legal advice. The two primary reasons for examining hypothetical religion-based charter schools are their inevitability and their uniqueness. The hypothetical format is used because it would be very difficult, if not impossible, to find an existing religion-based charter school. The exiting charter schools are not going to address all the questions interesting to those interested in policy or starting a religious charter school. Even if parents are motivated by religious reasons, they have very powerful incentives to hide those motivations in order to get their charter application accepted. The theoretical format allows one to tinker with the situations in order to directly address the legal questions most interesting to those who would consider forming religion-based charter schools.

The three hypothetical situations are as follows: (1) a morally-based school founded by coreligionists, which forms because parents are unhappy with the values taught in public school; (2) a half-time secular school that exists to provide a noncontroversial secular education to children who attend religious school every day; and (3) a traditional religious school operated by a religious organization. Each hypothetical situation addresses specific questions that relate to the school's formation and operation. The answer to the questions raised by the hypothetical schools sometimes requires altering the fact pattern of the charter school's formation.

The questions posited by the hypothetical situations focus on practical aspects of founding and operating a charter school while also illustrating how charter schools shift the balance of power between the state and parents. The answers to these questions will illustrate that charter schools cannot be considered in terms of a religious organization's access to a state facility nor as a mere funding program. The answers also demonstrate that parents can create charter schools that accommodate their religious beliefs, but not such schools that endorse their religion.

The seven questions addressed by the morally-based school generally address the issues of formation, mission, and control over the staff. Those questions are the following: (1) Can coreligionists form a charter school? (2) Can morality-based general propositions of good be taught in a charter school? (3) Can a charter school teach values espoused by coreligionists? (4) Can a charter school teach a course in the relationship between religion and morality? (5) Can a charter school have religious criteria for staff? (6) Can a charter school limit a teacher's right to express different worldviews? (7) Can a charter school offer optional prayer?

The format of the section describing the half-time school is slightly different than the other two hypothetical situations because two Supreme Court cases, *McCollum v. Illinois* (1948) and *Zorach v. Clauson* (1952), have directly addressed this issue. Therefore, those two cases are discussed separately and in-depth. The focus of the four questions in this hypothetical is on the purpose behind forming such a school. This section also examines involvement of clergymen and religious organizations in a charter's formation and operation. Those questions are: (1) Can a charter school form for the purpose of allowing students' ease of access to religious education? (2) Can a charter school form to provide students, who would otherwise attend faith-based schools, with a free, secular public education? (3) Can clergy sit on the board of a charter school? (4) Can a charter school share facilities with a religious school?

The questions addressed by the final abstract charter school examine the inherent issues if a religious organization operated a charter school. These seven questions address the issue of whether a charter school can endorse religion or even proselytize. (1) Can a religious organization operate a charter school? (2) Can a charter school have religious criteria for admission? (3) To what extent can a religion class be taught in a charter school? (4) Can a charter school have required religious instruction? (5) Can a charter school have required religious exercises or worship? (6) Can a charter school identify with a denomination? (7) Can states exclude religious-based charter schools from forming?

Chapter five once again examines the legal and other contexts of charter schools, with the perspective gained by having examined the hypothetical situations. The chapter also summarizes all the answers to the questions found in chapter four. The basic findings are that a charter school can form to accommodate parents' religious beliefs; however, a charter school cannot endorse parents' religious beliefs.

Chapter five also raises questions for further research. The primary questions for further research are whether it is possible that charter schools are not in fact state actors and therefore would require a different constitutional analysis. Such an analysis would require a very close examination of every state charter statute. Because most if not all state charter statutes define charter schools as state public schools, the possibility that charter schools are not state actors seems too remote to examine. Finally, the conclusion considers the question of whether religion-based charter schools are a good solution to the parental disaffection with existing public schools; in other words, are charter schools a good way to adjust the balance between the power of the state and individuals?

CHAPTER 2

LEGAL BACKGROUND

The Establishment Clause

INTRODUCTION

Understanding the legal issues surrounding religion-based charter schools requires an in depth knowledge of the Establishment Clause of the U.S. Constitution. This chapter provides a general understanding of the religion clauses and then moves on to discuss the Establishment Clause in greater detail. It also includes key terms to understanding church/state constitutional issues. Finally this chapter examines the most recent Supreme Court cases that have examined the separation between church and state and also examines the implications those cases have for the prospect of religion-based charter schools.

The precise meaning of the Establishment Clause has eluded even the Supreme Court. In his dissent to *McCollum v. Board of Education* (1948), Justice Reed stated that a "rule of law should not be drawn from a figure of speech" (*McCollum v. Board of Ed.*, 1948, 333 U.S. 203, 247, Reed, J., dissenting). The figure of speech to which he referred, "the separation between church and state," has to a great extent guided Establishment Clause jurisprudence and is better recognized than the language of the

Religious Charter Schools: Legalities and Practicalites, pp. 17–58
Copyright © 2007 by Information Age Publishing
All rights of reproduction in any form reserved.

Establishment Clause itself. The late Chief Justice Burger wrote in *Lemon v. Kurtzman* (1971),

> Judicial caveats against entanglement must recognize that the line of separation, far from being a 'wall,' is a blurred, indistinct, and variable barrier depending on all the circumstances of a particular relationship. (403 U.S. 602, 614)

Part of the reason why the separation between church and state was important to the founders can be attributed to the near complete lack of separation between church and state that existed in parts of Europe in the seventeenth century. Indeed, Sweden only disestablished its ties to Lutheranism in the late 1990s. One clear example of the difference between the European and American notions of separation between church and state recently occurred in France, which banned religious apparel from public schools partly on the grounds of maintaining a separation between church and state in the public schools (Sciolino, 2004). At the same time, French private religious schools receive state funding.

Many of the early American settlements, though they established state churches themselves, were founded by religious minorities who fled the established churches of England, Ireland, and Scotland (Pfeffer, 1967). The religion clauses were enacted at least in part because the founding fathers were concerned with the power that an exclusive, national church would have (Cord, 1982, p. 3). Moreover, the First Amendment rests upon the premise that religion and government can work to achieve their aims if each is left free from the other within its sphere (*McCollum v. Board of Education*, 1948, 333 U.S. 203, 212).

Consequently, the separation between church and state has two major themes: preventing the church from exercising undue influence over the state and stopping the state from intruding upon the realm of the church. The two religion clauses of the First Amendment are tailored to these themes. First, "Congress shall make no law respecting an establishment of religion," thus preventing the church attaining sovereign power; second, "Congress shall make no law ... prohibiting the free exercise [of religion,]" thus preventing the state from unduly exercising its sovereign powers over the church (First Amendment, 1791).

In *Reynolds v. United States* (1878) and *Everson v. Board of Education* (1947), the Supreme Court wrote into the opinion Thomas Jefferson's famous phrase holding that "the clause against establishment of religion by law was intended to erect 'a wall of separation between Church and State" (*Everson*, 330 U.S. 1, 17, citing *Reynolds*, 98 U.S. 145, 164). Despite the requirement of separation, religion is a regular part of American government and political discourse. For example, opening legislative sessions of deliberative public bodies with prayer has been held a constitutional tradition of this country (*Marsh v. Chambers*, 1983, 463 U.S. 783, 786). Politicians regularly invoke the will of God in political messages (Carter, 1993, p. 67, citing President George H. W. Bush's invocation of God regarding the Gulf War). Presidents court evangelists for their political endorsements (Willis, 1990, p. 79).

Regardless of politicians' use of religious rhetoric or appealing to the devout for votes, the separation between church and state is ultimately defined by the Supreme Court. The Court has the power to interpret the Constitution (*Marbury v. Madison*, 1803), and is the final arbiter of the boundaries of the rights the Constitution endows to the people (*City of Boerne v. Flores*, 1997).

In *Lemon v. Kurtzman* (1971 the Court described the meaning of the Establishment Clause, explaining that it does more than prevent an "establishment" of religion.

> A law may be one 'respecting' the forbidden objective while falling short of its total realization. A law 'respecting' the proscribed result, that is, the establishment of religion, is not always easily identifiable as one violative of the Clause. A given law might not establish a state religion but nevertheless be one 'respecting' that end in the sense of being a step that could lead to such establishment and hence offend the First Amendment. (403 U.S. 602, 612)

Unfortunately, it is difficult to succinctly describe the Court's interpretation of the "blurred, indistinct, and variable barrier" that separates church and state (403 U.S. 602, 614).

The Establishment Clause requires that the state be neutral toward religion. The state can neither advance nor inhibit religion (*Rosenberger v. University of Virginia*, 1995). Thus, each state is limited in its relationship with religious schools and may not encourage or discourage their formation or influence their operation. Nor may states promote or disparage religion in public schools. There is, however, a precarious balance between the "high wall of separation" and the need for some association between the state and churches.

> And so far as interference with the 'free exercise' of religion and an 'establishment' of religion are concerned, the separation *must be complete and unequivocal*. The First Amendment within the scope of its coverage permits no exception; the prohibition is absolute. The First Amendment, however, *does not say that in every and all respects* there shall be a separation of Church and State. Rather, it studiously defines the manner, the specific ways, in which there shall be no concert or union or dependency one on the other. (*Zorach v. Clauson*, 1952, 343 U.S. 306, 312)

One might think that the issue of religion charter schools is simple. Public schools are prohibited from requiring prayer (*Lee v. Weisman*, 1992). State legislatures cannot require the posting of the Ten Commandments (*Stone v. Graham*, 1980) or that creationism be taught in schools (*Edwards v. Aguillard*, 1987). State buildings, including public schools, cannot display a crèche endorsing Christianity (*County of Allegheny v. ACLU*, 1989). Presumably, charter schools are similarly prohibited from doing these things. Consequently, it seems reasonable to conclude that religious charter schools are banned by the Constitution. Other cases, however, suggest that the Constitution may not prohibit religious charter schools (*Board of Ed v. Grumet*, 1994; *Agostini v. Felton*, 1997; *Mitchell v. Helms*, 2000), and may even require that religious charters be allowed to form on an equal basis with secular ones. This case law bears closer scrutiny, which follows (*Good News Club v. Milford Central School*, 2001; *Rosenberger v. University of Virginia*, 1995).

A BRIEF INTRODUCTION TO THE RELIGION CLAUSES

The Establishment Clause and the Free Exercise Clause of the Constitution exist to protect the people's religious practices from the oppression of the government. The exact intentions of our founding fathers are, however, difficult to determine. Historians argue whether the Establishment Clause enacted the views of Thomas Jefferson, James Madison, or some other person such as Roger Sherman or Roger Williams (Cord, 1982; Levy, 1994; Pfeffer, 1967). Moreover, historians' interpretations of the views of Thomas Jefferson, who is often cited because he coined the term "wall of separation," are continually being revised (Goodstein, 1998).

This book will not attempt to resolve that debate, nor could it review the voluminous materials on the adoption and intention of the framers of the Establishment Clause. Regardless of the initial intention, it is clear that the scope of the Establishment Clause has changed in the past 200 years, just as the scope of other constitutional provisions such as the Cruel and Unusual Punishment Clause have changed. Though we may debate whether the Cruel and Unusual Punishment Clause has mutated enough to ban the death penalty, few, if any, would argue that it does not prohibit branding, butchering ears, or flogging which were common in 1791, when the Eighth Amendment was adopted (*Trop v. Dulles*, 1958; Woodward, & Armstrong, 1979, p. 207).

Moreover, the First Amendment originally only applied to the federal government. Any doubt that the Bill of Rights protected the people's rights from the federal government, not state governments, was settled in 1833 by *Barron v. Mayor and City Council of Baltimore*, which held that the

Fifth Amendment did not apply to the states. Subsequent Supreme Court decisions, however, have held that the Fourteenth Amendment, passed in 1868, applied both the Free Exercise Clause and the Establishment Clause to the states (*Cantwell v. Connecticut*, 1940; *Murdock v. Pennsylvania*, 1943).

The Establishment Clause prevents the state from establishing religion or respecting an establishment of religion. The Supreme Court has held that respecting an establishment means much more than setting up a state church. Justice Goldberg noted, in *School Dist. of Abington v. Schempp* (1963), "True religious liberty requires that government neither engage in nor compel religious practices, that it effect no favoritism among sects or between religion and nonreligion, and that it work deterrence of no religious belief" (374 U.S. 203, 305, Goldberg, J., concurring). The Establishment Clause and Free Exercise Clause have different standards. The standard, known as the *Lemon* test, fashioned by the Supreme Court for Establishment Clause cases, has three components and is discussed below.

THE FREE EXERCISE CLAUSE

The test used in Free Exercise Clause cases depends on the nature of the activity and the state's reasons for regulating the activity. The government cannot ever compel a belief (*West Virginia v. Barnette*, 1943). However, when government regulates an activity that is performed or banned by a religious organization, the test used to decide its constitutionality depends on two factors: the motivation behind the government's regulation and whether additional constitutional rights are implicated.

If the government is specifically targeting an activity performed or banned by a particular religious group, the government must have a compelling reason for doing so (this is known as strict scrutiny) (*Church of Lukumi Babalu Aye, Inc. v. City of Hialeah*, 1993). If, however, the government is regulating a general activity and its regulation of a religious activity is incidental, the regulation is constitutional unless applying the regulation to the religious adherent would be irrational (*Employment Div., Dept. of Human Resources of Oregon v. Smith*, 1990). When an additional constitutional right is implicated by the regulation, then the government must have a compelling reason for applying that regulation to the religious dissenter (*Wisconsin v. Yoder*, 1972).

Therefore, any analysis of a free exercise claim involves three distinct questions: (1) is the state compelling a belief; (2) is the state targeting a religious minority or is the law one of general application; and (3) are additional constitutional rights implicated.

THE ESTABLISHMENT CLAUSE

From *Everson* to the *Lemon* Test

Everson v. Board of Education (1947) is the seminal Establishment Clause case. Its holding, allowing New Jersey to fund transportation to religious schools, is not as important as the propositions it set forth. *Everson* applied the Establishment Clause to the states and spoke of the Establishment Clause in strict separationist terms, firmly writing Jefferson's wall metaphor into its opinion 330 U.S. 1, 15–16, citing *Reynolds v. U.S.*, 1878, 98 U.S. 145, 164.

The second seminal Establishment Clause case, *Lemon v. Kurtzman* (1971), set forth the *Lemon* test, which was used in almost every Establishment Clause case for the 30 years that followed. Again, the holding of *Lemon*, invalidating salary supplements to faith-based schoolteachers, is not as important as the standard that it set forth. The *Lemon* test fashioned by the Supreme Court for Establishment Clause cases has three prongs:

> the statute must have a secular legislative purpose; its principal or primary effect must be one that neither advances nor inhibits religion; and the statute must not foster an excessive government entanglement with religion. (403 U.S. 602, 612–13)

The *Lemon* test has been criticized by many justices—Justice Scalia compared it to a ghoul in a late-night horror movie (*Lamb's Chapel v. Center Moriches*, 1993). Until recently, the Supreme Court more or less consistently used it to decide all Establishment Clause cases since 1971.

Agostini v. Felton (1997), which will be discussed in greater detail later in this chapter, changed the form, but not the content, of the *Lemon* test. Although they are separate aspects of the *Lemon* test, effect and entanglement are of course interrelated: Consequently, a plurality of the Court in *Agostini*, contracted to two the number of prongs of the *Lemon* test, "It is simplest to recognize why entanglement is significant and treat it … as an aspect of the inquiry into a statute's effect" (521 U.S. 203, 206). However, *Agostini* did not change the substance of the *Lemon* test since religious entanglement is still prohibited, even though it is now considered, by a plurality of the Court, as part of the test for religious effect.

The Different Types of Establishment Clause Cases

For the purposes of this analysis, I have divided Establishment Clause cases into four general categories (see Table 2.1). Over 90% of the Court's cases for the past 30 years can be placed in one of these categories.

The first and second types of cases are interrelated, as aid to religious schools is a benefit given to religious organizations. Aid to schools is its own category because of the sheer number of cases, 30 since 1973, compared with other benefit and burden cases, 10 in the same amount of time. Both of these types of cases generally implicate both the primary effect and excessive entanglement prongs of the *Lemon* test. (I discuss entanglement as a separate prong because most of those cases occurred before *Agostini v. Felton*.)

The *Lemon* test works most effectively when examining government subsidies and other aid to religious organizations. The test enables the Court to consider whether a program is a general entitlement program or if it acts as a subsidy to religious institutions. Constitutional benefits given to religious organizations and schools include property tax exemptions for religious organizations, and neutral aid to religious organizations as

Table 2.1. The Four Types of Establishment Clause Cases

Type of Case	*Examples*	*Prong(s) of the Three-Part Lemon Test and Trend in the Courts*
1. Benefits and burdens to religious organizations and groups	*Bowen v. Kendrick*, 1988 (grants to family planning organizations); *Texas Monthly v Bullock*, 1989 (tax exemptions for religious periodicals)	effect mixed; depends on the degree of the effect
2. Aid to faith-based schools	*Sloan v. Lemon* (1973) (tuition reimbursements); *Mitchell v. Helms* (2000) (equipment loans)	effect; sometimes entanglement mixed, generally constitutional
3. Religious activities by the state	*Lee v. Weisman*, 1992 (prayer at graduation by invited clergy); *Santa Fe v. Doe*, 2000 (school policy of students voting about prayer at graduation)	purpose or effect generally unconstitutional
4. Access to state facilities by religious organizations	*Rosenberger v. University of Virginia*, 1995 (Christian student publication's use of general funds); *Good News Club v. Milford Central School*, 2000 (after-school religious club); *Locke v. Davey* (2004) (scholarship for devotional theology student)	Free Speech protection of activity; Free Exercise Clause protection of the activity generally constitutional if Free Speech protects the activity; probably not if it is only the Free Exercise Clause

part of a general aid program, for example, grants to religious organizations that provide family counseling, textbook loans to faith-based schools, grants to religious colleges, and on site speech, hearing and diagnostic services at faith-based schools, and equipment loans to faith-based schools (*Board of Education v. Allen*, 1968; *Bowen v. Kendrick*, 1988; *Mitchell v. Helms*, 2000; *Roemer v. Board of Pubic Works*, 1976; *Walz v. Tax Com. of the City of New York*, 1970; *Wolman v. Walter*, 1977).

Unconstitutional benefits to religious organizations and schools include sales tax exemptions for religious periodicals, salary supplements for teachers, and maintenance and repair grants for private schools, regardless whether those benefits are part of a general aid program (*Texas Monthly, Inc. v. Bullock*, 1989; *Lemon v. Kurtzman*, 1971; *Committee for Public Education v. Nyquist*, 1973). Many school-aid programs violate both the effect and entanglement prongs. In the past, the Court assumed that an aid program found unconstitutional under the primary effect prong could not be cured with appropriate oversight procedures because those procedures would involve excessive entanglement (*Aguilar v. Felton*, 1985). The Court's decision in *Agostini v. Felton* (1997), however, casts doubt on that assumption by limiting the factors the Court considers to be entangling.

Aid to elementary and secondary education often seems as if it is judged under a stricter standard than aid to other religious organizations. The Court, however, uses the same standard, the *Lemon* test, to decide the constitutionality of aid to schools and to other religious organizations. The Court has often used different assumptions when deciding aid-to-schools cases than other aid cases.

In the past, the great majority of private schools eligible for state aid were Catholic since in many states over 90% of private schools were Catholic schools. This is not the case for other state aid programs that benefit private, including religious, beneficiaries (*e.g.*, *Bowen v. Kendrick*, 1988). In *Lemon*, the Court used the assumption that parochial schools constituted an integral part of the religious mission of the Catholic church. Because of the numerical disparity and the assumption about mission, the starting point for analysis in school-aid cases was that funding private schools was funding the mission of Catholicism. This may explain why the disparity exists between cases that examine aid to elementary and secondary schools and cases involving aid to other religious organizations.

In 1975, then Justice Rehnquist pointed out the flaw in that starting point: because the state funds all public education, faith-based schools are a minor part of any aid program (*Meek v. Pettinger*, 1975). The constitutionality of religion-based charter schools may depend on whether the Court uses the traditional starting point of school-aid cases (i.e., funding the school equals funding a church's religious mission).

The third category of cases is those in which the state engages in religious activities. These activities are generally unconstitutional because they often violate the purpose prong of the *Lemon* test. Examples include compelling public schools to post the Ten Commandments on classroom walls, requiring an oath to hold government office, beginning each school day with a Bible reading or religious invocation, and requiring that creationism be taught with the theory of evolution (*Abington Twp. v. Schempp*, 1963; *Edwards v. Aguillard*, 1987; *Engel v. Vitale*, 1962; *Stone v. Graham*, 1980; *Torcaso v. Watkins*, 1961).

Some religious activities, such as some holiday displays, may they have a secular purpose, but an unconstitutional effect (*County of Allegheny v. ACLU*, 1989; *Lynch v. Donnelly*, 1984). Not all religious activities by the state violate *Lemon*'s purpose prong. States may open legislative sessions with a prayer (*Marsh v. Chambers*, 1983) or display signs that say "Happy Holidays" and even may, in some situations, display a nativity scene (*Lynch v. Donnelly*, 1984). Display of the Ten Commandments on public property is discussed below.

The final category of Establishment Clause cases is the use of state facilities by religious organizations. Not only does the Establishment Clause allow this activity, the Free Speech Clause of the Constitution prohibits the state from banning religious groups from using its property as long as two things apply. First, those groups must fit the neutral criteria for using the facilities. Second, allowing the group to use the facilities must not appear to endorse religion (*Lamb's Chapel v. Center Moriches*, 1993). Religious groups' right to free speech is no more or less protected than other groups' similar rights (*Widmar v. Vincent*, 1981; *Rosenberger v. University of Virginia*, 1995).

In the field of education, the risks of funding religious schools are far fewer than the risks posed by allowing religion into public schools. Funding or giving other benefits is far less invidious than the state promoting a religion, religion generally, or nonreligion. Funding does not put the state imprimatur on religion so long as the benefits go to all schools. Funding merely allows individuals to use state funds to defer their own expenses.

For example if the state funded all education, including faith-based, through block grants, such funding would not endorse or put the state imprimatur on faith-based education. Although such a program would be unconstitutional (*Mitchell v. Helms*, 2000), the state would not be favoring any particular religion or favoring religion over nonreligion. On the other hand, if the state gave its official approval to faith-based schools by funding the schools of only one religion it would create the same problem as endorsing religion in public schools.

When the state promotes religion in public schools, it creates the far greater danger that the views of the religious majority will be imposed on religious minorities. Promoting religion in public schools poses a greater danger because the state, by controlling and running public schools directly, puts its imprimatur on any religious views taught there or expressed by teachers or the administration.

If a single public school puts a picture of Jesus on one of its walls, that act tells all the students and visitors that the state (in the form of that district or community) prefers Christianity to other religions (*Washegesic v. Bloomingdale*, 1993). Of course if the picture were part of a display of many important philosophers or leaders, then it would be constitutional.

The nineteenth century common school movement was characterized by the opposite viewpoint: funding faith-based schools was viewed as a more substantial danger to the common good than was endorsing religion in public schools. That perspective, when taken to the extreme, explains why funding is less invidious than government performing religious acts or making religious decisions itself. For example, in the mid-nineteenth century, Philadelphia, in the name of nonsectarianism, forbade the use of Catholic Bibles in public schools; only Protestant Bibles were allowed (Jorgensen, 1987, pp. 76-80). Thus, once religion is allowed into public schools it may be allowed to become orthodoxy. This is certainly far more problematic than merely funding sectarian schools, so long as all private schools are funded without reference to religion.

A more modern example is the state plan in *Santa Fe v. Doe* (2000), which is discussed in more detail below. A school district allowed students to vote whether prayer would occur at graduation or football games. The problem with such a program is twofold. First, the district is already endorsing prayer by holding the vote. Second, the minority religious students then must hear the prayer that the majority religious students have chosen.

Funding private religious activity does not pose these dangers. For example, the state may choose to set up a fund to allow all schools to buy posters. Religious schools may buy indoctrinating posters that they put in their classrooms. Students in those classrooms are not going to think that the state wants them to believe what is on the posters. Although they may become more likely to follow the tenets of their school's religion because the posters are there, they would not make the connection with the state.

If, however, the state chooses to put the Ten Commandments up in every classroom, then students seeing this are likely to think that this is the religious viewpoint that the state wants them to believe. In *Lee v. Weisman* (1992) the Court warned of the dangers of even a limited policy of pressuring students to maintain respectful silence during a state-sponsored prayer:

The undeniable fact is that the school district's supervision and control of a high school graduation ceremony places public pressure, as well as peer pressure, on attending students to stand as a group or, at least, maintain respectful silence during the invocation and benediction. This pressure, though subtle and indirect, can be as real as any overt compulsion. Of course, in our culture standing or remaining silent can signify adherence to a view or simple respect for the views of others. And no doubt some persons who have no desire to join a prayer have little objection to standing as a sign of respect for those who do. But for the dissenter of high school age, who has a reasonable perception that she is being forced by the State to pray in a manner her conscience will not allow, the injury is no less real. There can be no doubt that for many, if not most, of the students at the graduation, the act of standing or remaining silent was an expression of participation in the rabbi's prayer. (505 U.S. 577, 593)

When examining the constitutionality of religious charter schools, the question will arise whether the state is funding religion or the state is promoting religion itself. Religious charter schools are, however, something in between. A religion-based charter school is not a mere funding problem because charter schools are public schools. But it also may not be a problem in which a state promotes religion itself because a private organization, not the state, operates the charter school.

KEY TERMS

Neutrality: When the Court uses the term neutrality it means neutral as to religion. The Court has used the term at least as far back as the *Everson* decision: "so that the school can inculcate all needed temporal knowledge and also maintain a strict and lofty neutrality as to religion." Neutrality is often defined in the negative. A program is not neutral toward religion if it advances religion (*Rosenberger v. University of Virginia*, 1995, 515 U.S. 819, 840, see also *Lemon v. Kurtzman*, 1971). The Court, however, has moved away from a definition of neutrality that is based on whether the benefit offered by a program advances religion to whether the recipients are defined on the basis of religion. Thus, a program that does not define participants on the basis of religion is now considered neutral.

We have held that the guarantee of neutrality is respected, not offended, when the government, following neutral criteria and evenhanded policies, extends benefits to recipients whose ideologies and viewpoints, including religious ones, are broad and diverse. (*Rosenberger v. University of Virginia*, 1995, 515 U.S. 819, 839)

Neutrality toward religion, therefore, can mean that either a program does not define recipients on the basis of religion or that it does not advance religion.

Endorsement: The Supreme Court most clearly defined endorsement of religion in *Lynch v. Donnelly* (1984), which held that the exhibition of "Seasons Greetings" sign, Santa Clause, and a crèche did not violate the Establishment Clause:

> Endorsement sends a message to nonadherents that they are outsiders, not full members of the political community, and an accompanying message to adherents that they are insiders, favored members of the political community. (465 U.S. 668, 688)

Endorsement relates to both the purpose and effect prongs of the *Lemon* test:

> The purpose prong of the Lemon test asks whether government's actual purpose is to endorse or disapprove of religion. The effect prong asks whether, irrespective of government's actual purpose, the practice under review in fact conveys a message of endorsement or disapproval. An affirmative answer to either question should render the challenged practice invalid. (465 U.S. 668, 690)

Therefore a government act endorses (or disapproves of) religion when either the purpose of the act is to convey a religious (or antireligious) message or the act has the effect of conveying such a message.

Separationism: The term separationism (sometimes called strict separationism) refers to the belief that government should maintain a strict separation between church and state. The term is derived from the famous statement about "separation between church and state" by Thomas Jefferson, which the Supreme Court wrote into law (*Everson v. Board of Ed of Ewing Twp.*, 1947, 330 U.S. 1, 17). Separationists are more likely to find that a program unconstitutionally advances or inhibits religion.

Accommodation/Accommodationism: The Establishment Clause does not prohibit the government from reasonably accommodating religious beliefs (*Board of Education v. Grumet*, 1994, 512 U.S. 687, 706). The main way that the state accommodates religious beliefs is by "alleviating special burdens." An example of a constitutional accommodation is that the government may allow religious organizations to favor their own adherents in hiring, even for secular employment (*Corporation of Presiding Bishop v. Amos*, 1987).

Accommodationism is the opposite of separationism. Accommodationist judges are more likely to find that a government program that advances religion is a permissible accommodation of religious beliefs, and less likely to find an Establishment Clause violation.

Nonfunding Principle: The principle established in *Everson* (1947) and solidified in the 1970s that established that it was generally inappropriate for the state to directly provide aid to religious organizations. This principle has been abandoned in favor of allowing aid so long as the beneficiaries are defined along neutral criteria and the benefits don't directly aid an organization's religious mission (*Mitchell v. Helms*, 2000).

Access/Limited Public Forum: Access is generally understood in terms of access to a limited public forum. A limited public forum is a venue for expression that is established by the state. The state may place reasonable time, place and manner restrictions on such a forum (*Lamb's Chapel v. Center Moriches*, 1993). The state may also narrowly define the content or topics that are included and excluded in the forum; however, the state cannot restrict a viewpoint from the forum. Therefore, the religious viewpoint may not be excluded from a limited public forum, but in certain circumstances the topic of religion may be excluded. As a result a religious organization must be granted access to a limited public forum on an equal basis with nonreligious organizations (*Lamb's Chapel v. Center Moriches*). Such access is always granted on the basis of the organization's right to free speech.

Per-capita Aid and Private Choice Programs: One of the key distinctions made in *Mitchell v. Helms* (2000), which is discussed below, is the distinction between per-capita aid programs and private choice programs. Unfortunately, Justice O'Connor, who discusses the distinction, does not describe what the difference between the two types of programs is. The primary difference between a private-choice program and a per-capita aid program, according to Justice O'Connor (and Justice Breyer who joined her opinion) seems to be the way the aid flows to the beneficiary; if the aid flows through the choice of a beneficiary then the aid is a private choice program.

This distinction is unsatisfying because any block grant based on the number of pupils attending a school is in actuality based on the choice of the student (or parents) who chose to attend that school. In *Mitchell* (2000), the aid went directly to the school; however, Justices O'Connor and Breyer found the program to be a private choice program because the students were eligible for the aid regardless of what school they attended, even though the aid went to the school.

A more reasonable distinction would be based on the form the aid takes. For example a voucher is given to the parent or student. The parent then chooses to give the aid to the school. This is private choice. A program that gives aid directly to the school is more reasonably interpreted as a per-capita aid program. Another way of viewing the distinction would be whether the religious effect was directly dependent on the private choice.

RECENT SUPREME COURT DECISIONS

The first part of this chapter gave an overview of the Establishment Clause. The two most important Establishment Clauses cases of this century were *Everson v. Board of Education* (1947), which applied the Establishment Clause to the states, and *Lemon v. Kurtzman* (1971). *Lemon* laid out the three part test used in nearly every Establishment Clauses case until 1997: (1) whether the statute has a secular legislative purpose, (2) whether the principle or primary effect is to advance or inhibit religion, and (3) whether the statute creates and excessive entanglement with religion.

There are four different types of Establishment Clause cases: (1) cases that examine benefits and burden to religious organizations; (2) aid to faith-based schools; (3) religious activities by the state; and (4) access to state facilities by religious organizations. Recent jurisprudence has moved away from examining these cases under the *Lemon* test and only examine the purpose and effect of a statutory scheme. Additionally, the means of examining the benefits to religion has changed. Originally the neutrality of a program was determined by whether it advanced or inhibited religion. Recent cases, when determining neutrality, look at whether the program defines the recipients on the basis of religion.

The following Supreme Court decisions are the Court's most recent major pronouncements on the Establishment Clause, taken together these cases clarify the current Court's understanding of the separation between church and state. Each of the cases is also cited when discussing the hypothetical situations in chapter four. The ensuing descriptions merely describe the cases and do not express the relationship between them and religious charter schools except in the most general terms.

Rosenberger v. University of Virginia (1995).

The University of Virginia finances the publications of its student groups using a special fund, the Student Activities Fund (SAF). A student group must become a Contracted Independent Organization (CIO) in order to use the SAF. Any student group with a majority of student members, whose managing officers are students, and that complies with other university requirements, can become a CIO. The SAF does not pay the groups directly, but pays contractors and creditors after a group submits a bill if the bill falls under the category of allowable activities, which includes printing group publications. The Wide Awake Project (WAP), a qualified, religious, Christian, student group, had its request for payment to its contractor refused solely because the group published a religious newsletter. The University maintained that the Establishment Clause prevented it from paying for the publication of the newsletter.

The Court first examined whether the Free Speech Clause of the First Amendment protected the student publication. The Court refused to distinguish between a state actor (i.e., the university) that grants a group access to its facilities and a state actor that gives a group financial reimbursement for its activities. In *Lamb's Chapel v. Center Moriches* (1993), the Court had unanimously held that a state actor, a school district, could not refuse after-hours access to a religious group once it had allowed other groups similar access to its facilities.

In *Rosenberger* (1995), the Court noted that access requires some amount of cost if only in terms of electricity and maintenance; thus, there was no constitutional reason to differentiate between physical access and financial reimbursement under the Free Speech Clause. The Court observed that the constitutional requirements of a state actor did not affect the University's since the funded publication was a student publication, not a university one. Consequently, the WAP had a right under the Free Speech Clause to equal access to the funds since denying those funds on the basis of religion was unconstitutional viewpoint-based discrimination.

The Court next examined whether the Establishment Clause prevented the University from funding the student publication. Before examining whether such funding would be constitutional the Court noted general principles of the Establishment Clause.

> A central lesson of our decisions is that a significant factor in upholding governmental programs in the face of Establishment Clause attack is their neutrality towards religion.... We [have] cautioned that in enforcing the prohibition against laws respecting establishment of religion, we must "be sure that we do not inadvertently prohibit [the government] from extending its general state law benefits to all its citizens without regard to their religious belief." We have held that the guarantee of neutrality is respected, not offended, when the government, following neutral criteria and evenhanded policies, extends benefits to recipients whose ideologies and viewpoints, including religious ones, are broad and diverse. (515 U.S. 819, 839, citing *Everson v. Board of Education*, 1947 and *Board of Education v. Grumet*, 1994)

The Court then found that the university funding program was neutral toward religion since there was no suggestion that the University established it for the purpose of funding religious publications. The SAF was established to create a forum for students, while recognizing the diverse nature of those interests. The Court noted a number of safeguards that guaranteed the neutrality of the program. First, the money went into a fund that could not be used for supporting a religion, but only to fund student publications. Second, the money went to private contractors rather than the student groups themselves. Third, the university, by creating a separate fund, separated itself from the speech.

> [Thus], the program respects the critical difference "between government speech endorsing religion, which the Establishment Clause forbids, and private speech endorsing religion, which the Free Speech and Free Exercise Clauses protect." (*Rosenberger v. University of Virginia*, 1985, 515 U.S. 819, 841 quoting *Board of Education v. Mergens*, 1990)

The Court refused, as it had in *Widmar v. Vincent* (1981), to make a distinction between speech about religion and religious speech. Both types of speech are equally protected by the Free Speech Clause and there was not enough of a risk of an Establishment Clause violation to try and attempt to draw such a line. Moreover, attempting to articulate such a line would involve the sort of government involvement that the entanglement prong of *Lemon* forbids. There was no Establishment Clause violation in the University funding the program that the Free Speech Clause required.

Rosenberger (1985) is important because it held that funding the student publication was not only constitutional, but also *required* by the Free Speech Clause. As a result *Rosenberger* presents an argument that the Constitution requires the state to allow religious charter schools to form. As is discussed at the end of chapter four, this is an argument that will almost certainly fail since charter schools are not likely to be considered speech. The case also may represent an inclination that certain religious charter schools would be found constitutional.

The decision was not decided as a funding case; it was decided as an of access case.

> It does not violate the Establishment Clause for a public university to grant *access* to its facilities on a religion-neutral basis to a wide spectrum of student groups, including groups which use meeting rooms for sectarian activities, accompanied by some devotional exercises.... The *error* made by the Court of Appeals, as well as by the dissent, *lies in focusing on the money* that is undoubtedly expended by the government, rather than on the nature of the benefit received by the recipient. (515 U.S. 819, 842)

If this analysis were applied to charter schools, the question would not be examined purely in terms of the funding of charter schools, but rather in terms of the type of benefit the charter school received.

Access rather than funding, is another way that charter schools are different from vouchers. Vouchers give money to a parent or institution, purely a financial issue. Charter schools give the parents a sort of access to run a school. Courts of course are free to view charter schools purely in financial terms, but *Rosenberger* (1995) may indicate a willingness on the part of a majority of the Supreme Court to look beyond the financial issue, to the deeper philosophical issue that is the nature of the benefit.

One of the purposes of charter schools is to give individuals the opportunity to create distinctive schools. The state may be creating a limited public forum, which is an area in which the state creates Free Speech right even though it wouldn't exist without state action. Examples of limited public fora are some student-run newspapers, public bulletin boards, and some public parks. The forum is not defined by what it is (e.g., a bulletin board or a park), but how the state defines its use. "The Constitution forbids a state to enforce certain exclusions from a forum generally open to the public even if it was not required to create the forum in the first place" *Perry Education Assoc. v. Perry Local Educators' Assoc.*, 1983, 460 U.S. 37, 45).

Once the state opens the forum to all, it cannot restrict its use by reference to the speaker or user's viewpoint. Thus, the traditional free speech protections would apply to charter schools if the state created charter schools as limited public fora. It is more likely, however, that the requirements of *Rosenberger* (1995) are not applicable to charter schools and, therefore, the Free Speech right does not apply to charters (*Bagley v. Raymond*, 1999). Even so, parents' right to educate their children may be enough to trigger *Rosenberger*'s requirement of equal access. Parental rights, however, do not have the same level of constitutional protection as free speech rights.

Agostini v. Felton (1997)

After the Supreme Court's 1985 decision in *Aguilar v. Felton*, the District Court in New York City entered a permanent injunction prohibiting the New York City Board of Education from using Title I funds to provide counseling or teaching services on private religious school grounds. In 1995, parents of students at faith-based schools petitioned the District Court to remove the injunction arguing that the Court's subsequent jurisprudence had eroded the Establishment Clause to the extent that the principles behind the injunction were no longer valid law. After the District Court rejected the argument and the Court of Appeals affirmed, the Supreme Court in *Agostini v. Felton* reexamined New York's potential use of Title I funds on site at faith-based schools, rather than requiring that those services take place off site, generally in mobile units.

The Court in *Agostini* (1997) announced that fundamental changes in Establishment Clause jurisprudence had taken place that required the overruling of *Aguilar v. Felton* (1985) and *Grand Rapids v. Ball* (1985). The Court first acknowledged, as *Aguilar* and *Grand Rapids* did, that the programs had a secular purpose. The Court then reviewed the assumptions upon which *Aguilar* and *Grand Rapids* were based.

Grand Rapids (1985) held that remedial counseling programs on faith-based school grounds had the primary effect of advancing religion for three reasons. First, teachers may inadvertently inculcate religious beliefs because of the pervasively religious environment. Second, the presence of public school teachers on faith-based school grounds created a symbolic union between church and state. Third, the program financed the religious mission of the school by paying for its secular activities. *Aguilar* (1985) held that attempting to prevent inculcation or a symbolic link through monitoring would create an excessive entanglement between church and state. The Court attacked all those reasons.

Earlier court decisions abandoned the presumption that placing a public employee on faith-based school grounds inevitably results in inculcation because of the pervasive sectarian atmosphere of the school. The Supreme Court held that such a placement does not create a symbolic link between church and state. Since the placement of a state-paid, sign language interpreter on faith-based school grounds did not create such a problem, placing a teacher or counselor would not necessarily do so. A state-paid employee is presumed to fulfill his or her duties in a religiously neutral manner.

Next, the Court noted that Title I services provided to faith-based schools do not relieve faith-based schools of costs they would have otherwise born because Title I services are necessarily "supplemental to the regular curricula." (521 U.S. 203, citing 34 C.F.R. § 200.12(a), 1996).

Moreover, although the school, not the students, applies for the Title I services, the services are provided directly to the students without any funds reaching the schools. Most importantly, as the provision of Title I services off campus has been held constitutional, the location where the students are provided the services would not affect the benefit given to the school.

Finally, in examining the effect of Title I, the Court acknowledged that a program that created an incentive to undertake sectarian education would be unconstitutional. However, the Court found that Title I creates no such incentive because the funds are available on a neutral basis to all children.

When it examines whether a program creates an excessive entanglement between church and state, the Court considers factors similar to when it examines a program's impermissible effect, namely the nature of the aid and the resulting relationship. Only entanglement that is "excessive" is unconstitutional. In *Aguilar* (1985), the finding of excessive entanglement was based on three factors: the monitoring of Title I teachers to prevent Establishment Clause violations; administrative cooperation between the school and state; and the danger of political divisiveness over the issue.

The last two factors are irrelevant, the Court reasoned, as they exist regardless of the physical placement of the Title I teachers and counselors; the factors exist whether the teachers are in classrooms or mobile units. Because the assumption that Title I teachers may inculcate religion is no longer valid, pervasive monitoring is no longer necessary. There is no reason to expect that a monthly visit by a supervisor to make sure no inculcation was extant would create an excessive entanglement, especially since no entanglement existed in *Bowen v. Kendrick* (1988), in which more onerous burdens were placed on religious institutions. *Bowen* held the Adolescent Family Life Act constitutional even though it authorized grants to religious institutions.

Agostini (1997) is significant in relation to religious charter schools because the Court expressed doubt about the existence of a "symbolic link" between church and state when a public employee is on the grounds of a religious institution. This may indicate that a symbolic link would not exist between church and state when the state contracts with religious individuals to operate a school. Lastly, the Court also eliminated one of the common objections to church-state partnerships: the political divisiveness argument.

Agostini's (1997) importance to aid cases is difficult to underestimate. *Mitchell v. Helms* (2000) and *Zelman v. Simmons Harris* (2002) both rest squarely on the reasoning the Court used in *Agostini*. The importance of the decision is not found in the contraction of *Lemon* from three prongs to two since excessive entanglement is still prohibited.

The importance of *Agostini* (1997) is that it departs significantly from the nonfunding principle the Court set in the 1970s and 1980s. *Agostini* illustrates that in a general way the Court was willing to be more accommodationist than separationist. The analysis of *Agostini*, however, is not directly relevant to charter schools because charter schools are public schools. Consequently, religion-based charter schools will likely survive or fail depending on whether they are considered religious acts committed by the state. However even if charter schools are viewed as a funding mechanism, the importance of *Agostini* will lie not in itself, but rather in *Mitchell* (2000) and *Zelman* (2002), which rely heavily on *Agostini*'s reasoning.

Santa Fe v. Doe (2000)

The Santa Fe Independent School District had two similar policies dealing with prayer at football games and at graduation. Both policies had a two-tiered system where students would vote first whether there would be an invocation and second who would deliver it. The "Prayer at Football Games" policy authorized two student elections, first to determine whether invocations would be delivered before games and second to select the student to deliver them. The graduation policy had the senior class vote to determine whether an invocation would be delivered and by whom. Both policies allowed proselytizing, denominational prayer, but both had fallback provisions disallowing denominational prayer in case denominational or proselytizing prayers were found unconstitutional.

The Supreme Court found both policies unconstitutional because the school had not created a forum for the students and thus the policies were considered government speech and unconstitutional. Students are allowed to deliver religious messages in public fora created by a school. In fact, the right to deliver religious messages is protected by the Constitution. However, "[t]here is a crucial difference between government speech endorsing religion which the Establishment Clause forbids and private speech endorsing religion, which the Free Speech and Free Exercise Clauses protect" (*Board of Education v. Mergens*, 1990, 496 U.S. 226, 249). The Court held that the school policy did not protect private religious speech, but rather promoted public religious speech.

The school policy also impermissibly fostered the views of majority students rather than protected those of minority students. "Fundamental rights may not be submitted to a vote; they may not depend on the outcome of the election" (*Santa Fe v. Doe*, 2000, 530 U.S. 290, 305; *West Virginia v. Barnette*, 1943, 319 U.S. 624, 638).

The policy was unconstitutional in both venues. Not only did the school endorse religious speech, but also attendance at both graduation and football games was to a certain extent compulsory, compounding the constitutional problem. The compulsion of attendance at graduation was discussed previously in *Lee v. Weisman* (1992) and was not addressed by the Court here. As for the compulsion at football games, the Court noted that

> There are some students, however, such as cheerleaders, members of the band, and, of course, the team members themselves, for whom seasonal commitments mandate their attendance, sometimes for class credit. The [school] District also minimizes the importance to many students of attending and participating in extracurricular activities as part of a complete educational experience. (530 U.S. 290, 311)

The Court went further holding that the policy would be unconstitutional even if every high school student's decision to attend a home football game were purely voluntary. The Court was persuaded that the delivery of pregame prayer has the improper effect of coercing those present to participate in an act of religious worship. "The government may no more use social pressure to enforce orthodoxy than it may use direct means" (530 U.S. 312).

The decision in *Santa Fe v. Doe* (2000) was not unexpected considering the Court's precedents in *Lee v. Weisman* (1992) and *Texas Monthly v. Bullock* (1989). *Lee* held unconstitutional a graduation prayer at a public high school by an invited clergyman. *Texas Monthly* held unconstitutional a tax exemption for religious periodicals. The tax exemption in *Texas Monthly* impermissibly aided religion because it only applied to religious periodicals. It did not exempt from taxation periodicals from a philosophical perspective:

> It is possible for a State to write a tax- exemption statute consistent with both values: for example, a state statute might exempt the sale not only of religious literature distributed by a religious organization but also of philosophical literature distributed by nonreligious organizations devoted to such matters of conscience as life and death, good and evil, being and nonbeing, right and wrong. Such a statute, moreover, should survive Press Clause scrutiny because its exemption would be narrowly tailored to meet the compelling interests that underlie both the Free Exercise and Establishment Clauses. (*Texas Monthly*, 489 U.S. 1, 27, Blackmun, J. concurring)

Similarly, the school policy in *Santa Fe* (2000) would be constitutional if it allowed students to vote whether there would be any sort of speech before a graduation or a football game. The 11th Circuit found such an approach constitutional in *Adler v. Duval County School Board* (2000), which was decided 3 months before *Santa Fe*. *Santa Fe* gives charter schools (and all public schools) a clearer understanding of what sort of prayer is constitutional or unconstitutional at a public school.

Santa Fe (2000) is a very important case with regard to religion-based charter schools. The Court has shown that it is very unwilling to allow public school policies that encourage religion. Consequently, charter school policies cannot endorse or favor religion, but must only accommodate the students' beliefs.

Santa Fe (2000) stands firmly for the proposition that students, not the administration, must initiate any religious activity on public school grounds. The Court was entirely unsympathetic to the argument that attendance at football games is voluntary noting that "pregame prayer has the improper effect of coercing those present to participate in an act of religious worship" (*Santa Fe*, 530 U.S. 290, 312). As a result, even though choosing a charter school is voluntary on the part of parents, a school policy that endorses religion would still be unconstitutional.

Mitchell v. Helms (2000)

In 1997, in *Agostini v. Felton* (1997), the Supreme Court held constitutional using Title I funds to teach remedial classes on the premises of faith-based schools, rather than in nearby mobile units. Shortly after that decision, speculation began whether the Court would address the issue of aid based on chapter 2 of the Education Consolidation and Improvement Act of 1981 going to faith-based schools. (In 2000 and now, chapter 2 was (and is) technically subchapter VI of chapter 70 of 20 U.S.C., where it was codified by the Improving America's Schools Act of 1994, Pub.L. 103-382, 108 Stat. 3707. For convenience, the Court used the term chapter 2. Prior to 1994, chapter 2 was codified at 20 U.S.C. §§ 2911-2976 (1988)). Chapter 2 provides states with money to purchase various educational materials, which the state then loans to qualifying (poor) public and private schools.

The resources included library services and materials (including media materials) assessments, reference materials, computer software and hardware for instructional use, and other curricular materials (20 USC § 7351). The materials themselves were always secular, neutral, and nonideological. The Supreme Court had previously held that it was unconstitutional for states or school districts to loan any curricular materials, other than textbooks, to faith-based schools (*Meek v. Pettinger*, 1975; *Wolman v. Walter*, 1977). The Court in *Mitchell* held such loans constitutional, overturning those previous cases.

Although six justices agreed that the program was constitutional, no five could agree on reasoning. Thus, there was no opinion of the Court, only a plurality opinion. Justice Thomas delivered the "judgment" of the Court and delivered an opinion that Chief Justice Rehnquist and Justices Scalia and Kennedy joined. Justice O'Connor wrote an opinion concurring in the judgment, which Justice Breyer joined.

The Court did not address whether the statute had a secular purpose or whether it caused an excessive entanglement. Both the plurality and the concurrence relied heavily on *Agostini v Felton* (1997). The two opinions cite *Agostini* for the three primary criteria used to determine a statute's religious "effect:" (1) whether it results in indoctrination, (2) whether the recipients are defined by reference to religion, and (3) whether the program creates an excessive entanglement. The plurality, however, explicitly interpreted *Agostini* to mean that entanglement was merely an aspect of effect, and no longer was a separate prong as it was under the *Lemon* (1971) test.

The primary difference between the plurality, concurrence, and dissent was over the issue of whether it was constitutional to provide secular aid that could be diverted to religious purpose. Examples of divertible aid include maps, which can be used to teach history from a secular or religious perspective, and an overhead projector, which can be used for any purposes. Textbooks have traditionally been considered nondivertible aid and therefore it is constitutional to provide them to religious schools (*Board of Ed. v. Allen*, 1968; *Meek v. Pettinger*, 1975). Table 2.2 illustrates the differences of the various justices and opinions with regard to the issue of divertibility; the author of the opinion is listed first.

Because no five justices agree on this issue and the view of Justices O'Connor and Breyer was the moderate position, their position is currently the law. Thus, aid to a religious program that is itself secular is constitutional even if it is divertible as long as it is not actually diverted to religious purposes. Consequently, states may provide divertible resources such as maps or overhead projectors to faith-based schools as part of a neutral program; however, those schools cannot use those materials for religious purposes.

Experience, however, teaches that a plurality opinion is the one that is most often cited by later courts. Both the plurality opinion and the concurrence address two main issues: (1) whether the aid results in indoctrination; and (2) whether the recipients are defined by reference to religion. Although both opinions find that the recipients are not defined by reference to religion, they differ with regard to the issue of indoctrination.

The plurality's examination of the issues of (1) indoctrination and (2) defining recipients focuses on the neutrality of the program.

In distinguishing between indoctrination that is attributable to the State and indoctrination that is not, we have consistently turned to the principle of neutrality, upholding aid that is offered to a broad range of groups or persons without regard to their religion. If the religious, irreligious, and areligious are all alike eligible for governmental aid, no one would conclude

Table 2.2. Positions of the Factions in *Mitchell v. Helms* (2000)

Plurality: Thomas, Rehnquist, Scalia, Kennedy	Concurrence: O'Connor, Breyer	Dissent: Souter, Stevens, Ginsburg
Aid can be diverted to religious purpose, therefore, divertibility does not matter.	Aid can be divertible, but cannot be diverted to religious purposes.	Aid cannot be divertible to religious purposes.

that any indoctrination that any particular recipient conducts has been done at the behest of the government. For attribution of indoctrination is a relative question. If the government is offering assistance to recipients who provide, so to speak, a broad range of indoctrination, the government itself is not thought responsible for any particular indoctrination. (*Mitchell v. Helms*, 2000, 530 U.S. 793, 810-11)

According to the plurality, the fact that the chapter 2 aid goes to the school on the basis of numerous choices of pupils ensures neutrality. The students choose the school irrespective of the chapter 2 aid; the school receives and the school then receives the aid based on the number of eligible students that attend.

The mere fact that aid goes to a private school does not create a government incentive for a student to attend a faith-based school. The dividing line between direct and indirect aid used by the Court in the 1970s and 1980s is therefore no longer relevant. According to the plurality, the new distinction between constitutional and unconstitutional aid is between aid based on private and government-made choices. Aid based on private choices is constitutional, while aid based on government choices is unconstitutional. Consequently, the divertibility or even actual diversion of the aid is irrelevant to the plurality.

The issue is not divertibility of aid but rather whether the aid itself has an impermissible content. Where the aid would be suitable for use in a public school, it is also suitable for use in any private school. Similarly, the prohibition against the government providing impermissible content resolves the Establishment Clause concerns that exist if aid is actually diverted to religious uses. (*Mitchell v. Helms*, 2000, 530 U.S. 793, 822)

A concern for divertibility, as opposed to improper content, is misplaced not only because it fails to explain why the sort of aid that we have allowed is permissible, but also because it is boundless—enveloping all aid, no matter how trivial—and thus has only the most attenuated (if any) link to any realistic concern for preventing an "establishment of religion." (530 U.S. 793, 824)

In this view, the primary question is whether the aid is secular and whether the recipients are defined on the basis of religion generally. Therefore, it does not matter what the school does with the aid or if the school is pervasively sectarian. This is a necessary change because inquiring whether the school is pervasively sectarian is offensive to the plurality.

The offensiveness and absurdity of such an inquiry is clearly illustrated by a Ninth Circuit discrimination case, *E.E.O.C. v. Kamehameha Schools* (1993), which was not discussed by the plurality. The *Kamehameha* court examined whether a school's requirement that its teachers be Protestant was justified under the exceptions to Title VII. The court asked whether the institution at issue was truly religious and found that it was not, holding that a school could not require that all on-campus teachers be Protestant when the curriculum of the school did not propagate religion. "There is nothing to suggest that adherence to the Protestant faith is essential to the performance of this job" (990 F.2d 458, 466). The lesson of *Kamehameha* is that the legal autonomy of faith-based organizations depends in part on their "moral autonomy" and "distinctive character" (Glenn, 2000, p. 208). Courts should not be examining whether a school is religious *enough*.

According to the *Mitchell* (2000) plurality, the two factors in determining the constitutionality of a program are the neutrality of choice by the students or recipients and the secular nature of the aid. "Reduced to its essentials, the plurality's rule states that government aid to religious schools does not have the effect of advancing religion so long as the aid is offered on a neutral basis and the aid is secular in content" (530 U.S. 793, 837). The plurality holds that aid to a faith-based school is constitutional so long as the recipients of the aid are not defined on the basis of religion (i.e., the aid is neutral); this ruling would include any aid that goes to both public and private schools. The aid itself must also be secular in nature; aid is secular so long as it is suitable for use in public schools.

Justice O'Connor's concurrence was at least as important as Justice Thomas' plurality opinion because her and Justice Breyer's view have been more or less the law. Now that Justice O'Connor has retired and Chief Justice Rehnquist has been replaced by Chief Justice Roberts, it remains to be seen where the current Supreme Court will draw constitutional lines. Of course all cases previously decided remain valid precedent unless explicitly overturned.

The concurrence agrees that neutrality is an important criteria in determining an aid program's constitutionality, "Nevertheless, we have never held that a government-aid program passes constitutional muster solely because of the neutral criteria it employs as a basis for distributing aid" (*Mitchell v. Helm*, 2000, 530 U.S. 793, 839). Regardless of a program's neutrality, actual diversion of aid, even if it is secular, is unconstitutional.

The concurring justices, like the dissenters, disagree with the plurality's like treatment of private choice programs and per-capita-aid programs. For the concurring justices, only private choice programs are constitutional. A private choice program is one where the individual student has the benefit, in this case chapter 2 resources, which she takes with her to the school.

A per-capita aid program is one where the state bases the aid on the number of qualifying students attending the school.

> I do not believe that we should treat a per-capita-aid program the same as the true private-choice programs... First, when the government provides aid directly to the student beneficiary, that student can attend a religious school and yet retain control over whether the secular government aid will be applied toward the religious education. The fact that aid flows to the religious school and is used for the advancement of religion is therefore wholly dependent on the student's private decision. (*Mitchell v. Helm*, 2000, 530 U.S. 793, 842)

Moreover, the concurrence concludes that per-capita-aid programs and true private-choice programs create different perceptions whether the state is endorsing religion; per-capita aid programs endorse religion, while private-choice programs do not.

> In the former example, [per-capita aid programs] if the religious school uses the aid to inculcate religion in its students, it is reasonable to say that the government has communicated a message of endorsement... That the amount of aid received by the school is based on the school's enrollment does not separate the government from the endorsement of the religious message. The aid formula does not—and could not—indicate to a reasonable observer that the inculcation of religion is endorsed only by the individuals attending the religious school... In contrast, when government aid supports a school's religious mission only because of independent decisions made by numerous individuals to guide their secular aid to that school, no reasonable observer is likely to draw from the facts ... an inference that the State itself is endorsing a religious practice or belief. (530 U.S. 793, 843, quoting *Witters v. Washington Dept. of Serv. for the Blind*, 1986, 474 U.S. 481, 493)

The concurrence, however, still finds giving chapter 2 aid to religious schools constitutional. Chapter 2 funds are distributed on a neutral basis, do not reach the coffers of the school, are not used to supplant funds from other sources, and all materials must be secular and nonideological. The line drawn by other cases between textbooks and other instructional materials was irrational because textbooks could be as easily diverted to religious uses as other materials.

According to the concurrence, the constitutional issue is whether materials are actually diverted to religious purposes. With regard to chapter 2 aid, the safeguards against diversion are constitutionally sufficient because one can generally trust religious teachers not to use the subsidized material for religious classes one can the trust good faith of the participating schools. Lastly, the actual diversions to religious uses that occurred were de minimus. Consequently, including religious schools in the chapter 2 program is constitutional.

Mitchell (2000) has positive implications for charter schools. A religion-based charter school could participate in a neutral government aid program, just as any religious school may. The more interesting insinuation comes from the fact that at least four Justices view the secular nature of aid and the neutrality of the recipient class as dispositive of an aid program. Charter programs certainly apportion aid without reference to religion and certainly award aid that is itself secular (i.e., tuition grants that are used to operate a school).

Moreover, the fact that four Justices would allow aid to be actually diverted to religious instruction has profound implications for the possibility of a charter school running the secular half of a religious school's program. The fact that the concurrence disagrees with this assessment is of course dispositive of the legal issue. Justice O'Connor and Justice Breyer's distinction between per-capita-aid programs and true private-choice programs illustrates the legal difference between vouchers and charters.

Vouchers are a true private-choice program, where the money follows to the school through the individual. Reading just *Mitchell* (2000) would indicate that using vouchers at a religious private school would be constitutional according to the concurrence (as was found in *Zelman v. Simmons-Harris*, 2002 discussed below). However, the question of whether a charter program constitutes per-capita-aid requires a greater degree of analysis.

What would constitute a per-capita aid program rather than a private choice program is not clear. The program in *Mitchell* (2000) to a certain extent seems like a per-capita program—the aid is given to schools on a per-capita basis based on the number of chapter 2 eligible students who choose to attend the school.

Justice O'Connor, however, bases her reasoning on the fact that the student is eligible for the funding based on income, regardless of the school she chooses. A state in theory could provide material loans to all students. Moreover, although the student is the theoretical beneficiary, the form of the aid—money to purchase various educational materials such as library services, media materials, assessments, reference materials, computer software, and hardware—directly benefits the school.

The primary difference between a private-choice program and a per-capita aid program seems to be the beneficiary. Although Justice O'Connor also discusses the question of endorsement, the question of how the aid flows determines how she and Justice Breyer view the constitutionality of a program, particularly when the program involves monetary subsidies. A charter school is not a clear example of either a per-capita aid program or a choice program. The money goes to the charter school on the basis of enrollment; but the students choose to enroll in the charter school.

Good News Club v. Milford Central School (2001)

New York State law allows local school boards to adopt regulations regarding the use of school facilities after school hours (N.Y. Educ. Law § 414, 2000). Milford Central School adopted a policy authorizing district residents to use its building after school for, among other things, (1) instruction in education, learning, or the arts and (2) social, civic, recreational, and entertainment uses pertaining to the community welfare. Pursuant to Milford's policy, Stephen and Darlene Founier, sponsors of the Good News Club, a private Christian organization for children ages 6 to 12, submitted a request to hold the Club's weekly after-school meetings in the school. The club activities include games, reciting Bible verses, the telling of Bible stories, and prayer. The school denied their request. The Founier's sued.

The Supreme Court held that the free speech clause prohibited the school from banning religious, after-school clubs. Although two Justices wrote concurring opinions in *Good News Club* (2001), five Justices agreed upon a reasoning and there was a majority opinion. The two issues examined by the Court were as follows: (1) Is the speech at issue protected by the Free Speech Clause?; (2) Does the Establishment Clause prohibit the speech?

The parties agreed that the school created a limited public forum and the Court decided the case on that basis. A limited public forum is a forum that the state (in this case the school district) creates for a specific purpose and for specific individuals. The purposes of the forum in this case included "instruction in education, learning, or the arts and social, civic, recreational, and entertainment uses pertaining to the community welfare." The individuals included were residents of the district.

> When the state establishes a limited public forum, the state is not required to and does not allow persons to engage in every type of speech. The state may be justified in reserving [its forum] for certain groups or for the discussion of certain topics. The restriction must not discriminate against speech on the basis of viewpoint, and the restriction must be reasonable in light of the purpose served by the forum. (*Good News Club*, 2001, 533 U.S. 98, 106)

When presented with a limited public forum case, a court first asks, is the exclusion viewpoint discrimination? If yes, the exclusion is unconstitutional. If no, a court asks, is the limitation reasonable in light of the purposes of the forum? Here the Supreme Court found viewpoint discrimination so there was no need to ask if the restriction was reasonable.

There is no question that teaching morals and character development is a permissible purpose under the school regulations; the club was excluded because the school equated religious activities to religious instruction.

> The Club seeks to address a subject otherwise permitted under the rule, the teaching of morals and character, from a religious standpoint. Certainly, one could have characterized the film presentations in *Lamb's Chapel* as a religious use.... The only apparent difference between the activity of *Lamb's Chapel* and the activities of the Good News Club is that the Club chooses to teach moral lessons from a Christian perspective through live storytelling and prayer, whereas *Lamb's Chapel* taught lessons through films. This distinction is inconsequential. Both modes of speech use a religious viewpoint. Thus, the exclusion of the Good News Club's activities, like the exclusion of *Lamb's Chapel*'s films, constitutes unconstitutional viewpoint discrimination. (*Good News Club*, 2001, 533 U.S. 98, 109)

Similarly, as discussed above, *Rosenberger* (1995) held that religious speech is protected from viewpoint discrimination. The Court in *Good News Club (2001)* went so far as to say that actual religious worship was a religious viewpoint that could not be discriminated against.

> We disagree that something that is "quintessentially religious" or "decidedly religious in nature" cannot also be characterized properly as the teaching of morals and character development from a particular viewpoint.... What matters for purposes of the Free Speech Clause is that we can see no logical difference in kind between the invocation of Christianity by the Club and the invocation of teamwork, loyalty, or patriotism by other associations to provide a foundation for their lessons. (*Good News Club*, 2001, 533 U.S. 98, 111)

Because the school had no valid Establishment Clause interest, the Court did not address whether such an interest would outweigh the Free Speech Clause. The Establishment Clause was not implicated because there was no expectation that the club's speech would be attributed to the school.

The Court cites a number of factors including that the club is after school, the program is neutral toward religion, and the decision to form and attend the club was made by parents. Additionally, the danger of impressionability of children only exists when the activity takes place during school hours, not after. If there were a danger that children would perceive the club as endorsed by the school, there would be a related danger that banning the club would be perceived as denounced by the school.

Good News Club (2001) draws on the reasoning in *Rosenberger* (1995) and takes it one step further. Because in *Rosenberger* the issue was a student newspaper, the Free Speech issue was overt. Here the issue is the viewpoint of a club. It is easier to draw an analogy between a religious club using the school and a religious charter forming using a neutral state scheme.

There is of course a great difference between an after school club and a charter school. Because the religious club it occurs after school it was less likely to be perceived as endorsed by the school, and, therefore, the state. Unlike such a club, a religious charter would be the school. Therefore, there is a much greater danger that the children attending a charter school would perceive the school's religious message and character as endorsed by the state. *Good News Club* (2001) leaves the issue undecided because it specifically does not address whether a club (or a school) prohibited by the Establishment Clause would still be protected by the Free Speech Clause. Religious charter schools would require the state to balance the Free Speech Clause and the Establishment Clause in a unique way. *Good News Club* supports the argument that the Free Speech Clause allows or requires allowing religion-based charters, but it is certainly not dispositive of the issue.

Zelman v. Simmons-Harris (2002)

Before *Zelman* (2002), the constitutionality of including religious schools in voucher programs was unclear. Supreme Court cases from the 1970s seemed to indicate that including religious schools in voucher programs was unconstitutional, but never held so explicitly. Later Supreme Court cases built upon the room left by *Committee for Public Education v. Nyquist* (1973) and *Sloan v. Lemon* (1973) and held constitutional tax deductions for the costs of private schooling so long as the tax deductions are also available to students who attend public school (*Mueller v. Allen*, 1983). *Nyquist* and *Sloan* also left open the door for specifically targeted voucher programs (*Committee for Public Education v. Nyquist*, 1973, 413 U.S. 756, 782). Lower court cases indicated that programs that include both public and private (including both religious and nonreligious) schools are constitutional (see, e.g., *Jackson v. Benson*, 1998).

Ohio created the Ohio Pilot Projected Scholarship Program, a voucher program in the Cleveland City School District to serve the poor students in that failing school district. The program allows poor students to attend public schools in adjacent districts and private schools within the Cleveland School District. The Sixth Circuit Court of Appeals in *Simmons-Harris v. Zelman* (2000) held the Cleveland voucher program unconstitutional as applied to faith-based schools. The Sixth Circuit held the program violated the Establishment Clause despite a ruling by the Ohio Supreme Court (*Simmons-Harris v. Goff*, 1999) that including religious schools did not violate either state or federal Establishment Clauses.

The Supreme Court in *Zelman v. Simmons-Harris* held that including faith-based schools in the program was constitutional. Although two Justices (O'Connor and Thomas) filed concurring opinions, both Justices joined the majority opinion, which was delivered by Chief Justice Rehnquist. Consequently, the ruling in *Zelman* carries more force and is easier to understand than *Mitchell v. Helms* (2000).

The Ohio program provides two types of aid: tuition aid (vouchers) that allows students to attend schools of their parents' choosing; and tutorial aid for students who choose to remain in public school. Any private school, whether religious or nonreligious, may participate in the program, though they must agree not to discriminate against students on the basis of race, ethnicity, or religion. (Ohio Rev. Code Ann. § 3313.976). Public schools in districts adjacent to the Cleveland district who participate are eligible to receive a $2,250 tuition grant per pupil, in addition to the full amount of per-pupil funding attributable to each individual student (the exact amount was disputed).

The amount of the tuition grant for private schools depends on the income of the families and school tuition. Families with income below twice the poverty line are given priority and are eligible to receive up to 90% of the school's tuition, up to $2,250; private schools may not charge these families more than a $250 co-pay. The state of Ohio has also enacted other initiatives such as magnet schools and community schools that provide additional funding for students who attend these Cleveland district public schools. The program's constitutionality was attacked for its inclusion of private religious schools.

The Court noted the distinction between per-capita aid programs that provide aid directly to schools and true private choice programs that provides aid based on the choices of individuals. The Court then reviewed other private choice programs that have been before the Court. According to the Court, those cases stand for the following principle:

> [W]here a government aid program is neutral with respect to religion, and provides assistance directly to a broad class of citizens who, in turn, direct government aid to religious schools wholly as a result of their own genuine and independent private choice, the program is not readily subject to challenge under the Establishment Clause. (*Zelman v. Simmons-Harris*, 2002, 536 U.S. 639, 652)

Because the Cleveland program is based on the choices of individuals and does not define recipients on the basis of religion, the program is constitutional. The aid goes to the private religious schools based on the parents' decisions to send their children to a religious school.

> It is part of a general and multifaceted undertaking by the State of Ohio to provide educational opportunities to the children of a failed school district. It confers educational assistance directly to a broad class of individuals defined without reference to religion, i.e., any parent of a school-age child who resides in the Cleveland City School District. The program permits the participation of all schools within the district, religious or nonreligious. Adjacent public schools also may participate and have a financial incentive to do so. (536 U.S. 639, 653)

Consequently, there are no financial incentives that skew the program towards religious schools.

The aid is provided on the basis of neutral secular criteria that neither favor nor disfavor religion. The Court pointed out that the program created a financial disincentive for private schools since parents who send their children to private schools make a co-payment, while parents who send their children to district-adjacent public schools or magnet and community schools do not have a co-payment. However, this feature was not necessary for the program to be constitutional.

The Court rejected the argument that the program creates the perception that the state endorses religious beliefs.

> [N]o reasonable observer would think a neutral program of private choice, where state aid reaches religious schools solely as a result of the numerous independent decisions of private individuals, carries with it the imprimatur of government endorsement. (*Zelman v. Simmons-Harris*, 2002, 536 U.S. 639, 655)

Moreover, the Court noted that a range of secular educational opportunities remained for Cleveland students. Also rejected were the arguments based on statistical evidence. That 82% of Cleveland's private schools are religious and that 96% of the scholarship recipients enrolled at religious schools are irrelevant to the program's constitutionality. The fact that 82% of Cleveland's private schools are religious is wholly unrelated to the tuition aid program.

The Court also noted that less than 45% of private schools are religious in Maine and Utah, while over 90% of private schools are religious in Nebraska and Kansas. It would be illogical for a tuition aid program to be constitutional in one state, but not another. The argument based on 96% of the scholarship recipients attending religious schools ignores the aid provided to 1,900 students in community schools, 13,000 students enrolled in magnet schools, and 1,400 students who received tutorial aid.

Zelman (2002) was ground breaking in that no previous decision had ever held constitutional a voucher program that included religious schools. However, *Zelman* did not make any changes to existing law and was predicted after the Court's decision in *Agostini* (Weinberg, Russo, & Osborne, 1998). *Zelman* also did not settle the constitutionality of religion-based charter schools. The Court held that a participant-choice based aid program could provide a religious school with unrestricted funds in the form of a voucher.

However, *Zelman* (2002) did not address what the bounds of a choice based program are vis-à-vis a per-capita based aid program. Charter schools are funded in a significantly different way than vouchers; therefore, the constitutionality of vouchers for poor students (even if it were for all students) does not settle the issue. Moreover, because charter schools are public schools, funding is only one of many issues that applies to the constitutionality of religion-based charter schools.

Locke v. Davey (2004)

Locke v. Davey (2004) held that a state may exclude theology majors from a state scholarship program. Seven justices found the program exclusion constitutional. The state of Washington established the Promise Scholarship Program to assist students with postsecondary expenses; to be eligible for the program a student must meet certain academic, income and enrollment requirements and may not be pursuing a theology degree. The Washington Constitution provides, "No public money or property shall be appropriated for or applied to any religious worship, exercise or instruction, or the support of any religious establishment" (540 U.S. 712, 719, quoting, Washington Constitution, Art. I, § 11). All sides agreed that the Establishment Clause would allow the state to provide scholarships to theology students; however, the question was whether the state could exclude theology students from this otherwise neutral benefit program. The issue before the Court was whether the Free Exercise Clause required the state to provide scholarships to theology students.

The *Locke v. Dewey* (2004) Court noted that when the Establishment Clause permits a state action, but the Free Exercise Clause does not require such action, there is "play in the joints" (540 U.S. 712, 718). Such cases are often evident when "the link between government funds and religious training is broken by the independent and private choice of recipients" (540 U.S. 712, 719).

The primary reason that the state could refuse to provide devotional theology students from participation in the scholarship program is because historically the states have treated ministry education differently from other schooling. To support this contention, the Court noted that several states excluded only the ministry from state education grants from the nation's incipience. Because devotional education is qualitatively different from other graduate education, Washington could constitutionally exclude devotional theology students from participation in the scholarship program.

The Court also noted five secondary reasons for finding the exclusion of theology students from the program constitutional. First, the state was not imposing any sanctions on any religious service or rite. Second, the state did not deny ministers the right to participate in political affairs. Third, the state did not require students to choose between their religious beliefs and receiving a government benefit. Fourth, the state was merely choosing not to fund a distinct category of instruction. Fifth, the state has shown no hostility toward religion because it allows students to receive scholarships if they attend pervasively religious accredited colleges, but receive nontheology degrees.

The decision in *Locke v. Davey* (2004) was a narrow one. The conclusion was primarily based on the distinction between ministry education and other forms of education. As such it may have relatively little impact on the issue of the constitutionality of religion-based charter schools. If the decision had come out the other way, however, it would have had a profound impact on a denominational charter's ability to argue that it was unfairly excluded from the chartering process.

With regard to the prospect of religion-based charter schools, the secondary reasons articulated by the Court finding the exclusion constitutional, are more important than the primary reason it used. Parents who want to operate a religious charter school, but are prohibited from doing so by the state, are not being subjected to sanctions and are not being asked to choose between their religious beliefs and a government benefit. On the other hand, parents may be able to successfully argue that they are being denied the right to participate in political affairs (operating a charter school) or that excluding religion-based charter schools illustrates hostility toward religion (by banning denominational charter schools).

Perhaps the most important feature of *Locke* (2004) is the expansion of the principle of "play in the joints." It will remain to be seen what forms of religion-based charter schools will fall under this principle or what forms will be considered banned by the Establishment Clause. Lastly, it is important to note that *Locke* was only examined under the Free Exercise Clause, rather than the Establishment Clause or Free Speech Clause, and that Respondents were unable to articulate an argument that the scholarship was speech. This may indicate a difficulty later on articulating charter funding as speech.

Van Orden v. Perry (2005) and *McCreary County, Ky. v. American Civil Liberties Union of Ky.* (2005)

On June 27, 2005 the Supreme Court decided *Van Orden v. Perry* and *McCreary County, Ky. v. American Civil Liberties Union of Ky.* Both cases addressed the constitutionality of displaying the Ten Commandments on public property. The Justices referred to the two cases in their opinions, attacking the reasoning of one case in the other. Therefore, these two cases are discussed as a unit.

Briefly, *Van Orden* (2005) held that a monument containing the Ten Commandments that had been erected 40 years previously on the Texas State Capitol grounds was constitutional and did not have to be removed. *McCreary County* (2005) held that displays of the Ten Commandments erected by two Kentucky counties were unconstitutional and had to be removed. Both cases were decided by a five-four votes of the Supreme Court. The one justice who agreed with both Court decisions was Justice Breyer.

The facts of *Van Orden* (2005) are as follows. The 22 acres surrounding the Texas State Capitol contain 17 monuments and 21 historical markers. In 1961, the Fraternal Order Of Eagles of Texas, a national social, civic, and patriotic organization, presented the six-foot tall monument, which was accepted by the Texas state organization responsible for maintaining the Capitol grounds. The monument contains the text of the King James Version of the Ten Commandments, two Stars of David, the Greek letters Chi and Rho (the monogram for Christ) and a statement that the Eagles donated the monument to the children and people of Texas. Thomas Van Orden testified that he used the law library located on the capitol grounds beginning in 1995 and sued the State six years after he first came into contact with the monument.

Van Orden (2005) was decided by a plurality. Four justices signed the plurality opinion and Justice Breyer wrote a separate concurring opinion. The plurality began by noting the "two faces of the Establishment Clause;" one face looks "toward the strong role played by religion and religious traditions throughout our Nation's history" and the other looks toward "the principle that governmental intervention in religious matters can itself endanger religious freedom" (*Van Orden v. Perry*, 545 U.S. 677, 683).

> Reconciling these two faces requires that we neither abdicate our responsibility to maintain a division between church and state nor evince a hostility to religion by disabling the government from in some ways recognizing our religious heritage. (545 U.S. 677, 683-84)

The plurality then noted that the Court has used the Lemon test and other tests when examining Establishment Clause cases. The *Lemon* (1971) test was not useful in *Van Orden* (2005), and the plurality's analysis was driven by the nature of the monument and by our Nation's history.

The plurality then began a long examination of various religious acts in the nation's history, some of which were found constitutional by the Supreme Court and others of which were never challenged. Monuments to the role played by the Ten Commandments in our nation's heritage are common throughout America and the Ten Commandments has both religious and secular meanings.

The plurality then addressed *Stone v. Graham* (1980), which held unconstitutional a state statute requiring the posting of Ten Commandments in all public schools. *Stone* is viewed as an example of the particular vigilance utilized by the Court when in monitoring compliance with the Establishment Clause in elementary and secondary schools. The placement of the monument on the capitol grounds was also more passive than the posters at issue in *Stone*. Additionally, the fact that Van Orden himself walked past the monument for years before filing the lawsuit further demonstrated the monument's passivity. The plurality ended by noting that the monument was one of several included on the Texas capitol grounds and fit the neutral criteria set forth by the Texas legislature for such monuments.

Justice Breyer did not join the plurality decision. Because he was the most moderate vote, his concurring opinion has the force of law. He began his opinion by stating that the religion clauses of the First Amendment "seek to avoid that divisiveness based upon religion that promotes social conflict, sapping the strength of government and religion alike" (*Van Orden v. Perry*, 2005, 545 U.S. 677, 698).

Although the Establishment Clause prevents the government from "excessive interference with, or promotion of, religion, [it] does not compel the government to purge from the public sphere all that in any way partakes of the religious" (*Van Orden v. Perry*, 2005, 545 U.S. 677, 699). In Justice Breyer's view *Van Orden* is a borderline case with no test-related substitute for the exercise of legal judgment based on the underlying purposes of the religion clauses. The inherently religious text of the Ten Commandments does not by itself determine the case for Justice Breyer, but rather the context for that message is what is dispositive.

Here, the monument communicates a message that is both religious and secular. The circumstances surrounding the display's placement on the capitol grounds and its physical setting suggest that the state intended the nonreligious aspects of the monument's message to predominate. The fact that there were no complaints about the monument's message for 40 years demonstrates that the secular message in fact predominated. The donor organization, the Fraternal Order of the Eagles is a civic, primarily secular, organization whose interest in the Ten Commandments relates to the secular goal of preventing juvenile delinquency. The monument is one of 17 monuments and 21 historical markers on the capitol grounds. Justice Breyer went on to note that the monument was not in a school and, unlike *McCreary County* (2005), there was nothing in the history of the monument to indicate that it was placed there for religious purposes.

The facts of *McCreary County, Ky. v. American Civil Liberties Union of Ky.* (2005) are as follows. Two Kentucky counties, McCreary County and Pulaski County, each posted large, readily visible, farmed, abridged copies of the King James Version of the Ten Commandments, including citation to Exodus, in their courthouses. The ACLU sued.

After the suit was filed, but before a request for an injunction was heard, both counties enacted legislation and changed the display. The nearly identical resolutions called for a more extensive exhibit meant to show that the Commandments are Kentucky's "precedent legal code." The resolutions noted several grounds for taking that position, including the state legislature's acknowledgment of Christ as the "Prince of Ethics." The displays around the Commandments were modified to include eight smaller, historical documents containing religious references as their sole common element, for example, the Declaration of Independence's "endowed by their Creator" passage and the national motto, "In God We Trust" were included.

The Federal District Court entered an injunction requiring the counties to remove the displays. Subsequently, without changing the enabling legislation, the counties changed the displays again. The third displays were titled "The Foundations of American Law and Government Display" and consisted of nine framed documents of equal size. One of the nine documents sets out the Ten Commandments, explicitly identified as the "King James Version," quotes them at greater length than the prior displays, and explains that the Commandments have profoundly influenced Western legal thought and the United States. The other documents include the Star Spangled Banner's lyrics and the Declaration of Independence, accompanied by statements about their historical and legal significance.

Writing for the Court, Justice Souter held that the third displays had a religious purpose and were unconstitutional. The Court addressed two questions, first whether a determination of the religious purpose alone is a sound basis for ruling that the display violates the Establishment Clause; second, whether evaluation of purpose for the ultimate displays may take their evolution into account. The Court held that the manifest religious purpose required the removal of the display and that the evolution of the display could be taken into account when determining the display's purpose.

The majority's analysis began with *Stone v. Graham* (1980), which held unconstitutional a Kentucky statute that required all public schools to place posters with the Ten Commandments in classrooms. "*Stone* found a predominantly religious purpose in the government's posting of the Commandments, given their prominence as 'an instrument of religion' " (*McCreary*, 2005, 545 U.S. 844, 859). The two counties asked the Court to abandon the search for the purpose of the display, arguing that the purpose was unknowable. The counties argued in the alternative that any secular purpose would make the display constitutional even if there were an additional religious purpose.

The Court reaffirmed the purpose prong of the *Lemon* (1971) test, holding that whenever the state acts with a religious purpose it violates the principle of neutrality and, therefore, the Establishment Clause. The government may not favor religion over nonreligion because it sends a message to nonadherents that they are outsiders, not full members of the political community (545 U.S. 844, 860, quoting *Santa Fe v. Doe*, 2000). The Court wholly rejected the two counties' argument that the purpose was unknowable because examination of statutory purpose is a staple of appellate jurisprudence.

Examinations of statutory purposes in the context of the Establishment Clause do not require that judges or justices look into the hearts of legislators, but rather merely require that they objectively scrutinize the "text, legislative history, and implementation of the statute" (*McCreary County*, 2005, 545 U.S. 844, 862). The majority then noted how past Supreme Court cases examined text, legislative history, and implementation to determine whether various statutes had a secular or religious purpose. Such an inquiry is not "rigged in practice" to find a religious purpose (*McCreary County*, 545 U.S. 844, 863).

State action must have a genuine secular purpose that is not a sham. Although the government's stated purpose has some deference, courts must examine whether the stated secular purpose is merely secondary to a religious objective. To hold that any secondary secular purpose would suffice would render the purpose prong of the *Lemon* (1971) test meaningless. The counties' purpose must be looked at in the full context of the history of all three displays, not merely the context of the third, at-issue displays.

Stone (1980) held that the Ten Commandments is an instrument of religion. However, *Stone* did not hold that any display of the Ten Commandments by the state is unconstitutional. *Stone* held that the constitutionality of the display was determined by what the viewers would fairly understand to be the purpose of the display.

The display of the text of the Ten Commandments is of greater religious significance than the display of a representation of the tablets with Roman numerals because the text of many of the commandments is inherently religious, proclaiming, among other things, the existence of a monotheistic god. The displays at issue in *Stone* (1980) and the instant case contain the text of the actual commandments. The display in *Stone* and the first displays by the counties both set forth the text of the Ten Commandments without any context. When the text of the Ten Commandments is set forth by itself, its obvious religious message predominates.

Furthermore, the ceremony placing the first display in Pulaski County included a pastor, who testified to the certainty of the existence of God. "The reasonable observer could only think that the Counties meant to emphasize and celebrate the Commandments' religious message" (*McCreary*, 545 U.S. 844, 869). That the Ten Commandments have a relationship with secular law does not mitigate the fact that the text of the Commandments, when viewed alone, convey a clear religious message.

The Court then addressed the second and third displays. The two counties argued that the second display and its accompanying resolution were "dead and buried." The Court, however, held that the reasonable observer would be aware of this history, which made it relevant to the constitutional analysis.

The third displays were the counties' Foundations of American Law and Government exhibits, which included the Ten Commandments and other historical documents thought to be significant to the foundation of American government. The counties argued that the third displays had a secular purpose, which was "to educate the citizens of the county regarding some of the documents that played a significant role in the foundation of our system of law and government" (*McCreary*, 545 U.S. 844, 871). The court found that purported purpose was adopted for litigation purposes. Also, both lower courts rejected that ostensible purpose, finding that the government's purpose in putting up the display was religious. "No reasonable observer could swallow the claim that the Counties had cast off the objective so unmistakable in the earlier displays" (*McCreary*, 545 U.S. 844, 872).

Furthermore, the selection of the documents, which the Court discussed at length, did not articulate a common unifying secular purpose in light of the other important documents that were not displayed. For example, the third display had a long quote from the Magna Carta, but did not include this country's original constitution of 1787. Ultimately the Court held that the state's purpose needs to be taken seriously under the Establishment Clause and needs to be understood in light of the full context; an implausible claim that governmental purpose has changed does not change impermissible state action into constitutional action.

The Court next turned to the importance of neutrality in Establishment Clause jurisprudence. No one contends that the Establishment Clause only prohibits the establishment of a national church; the disagreement is over where establishment begins. The Establishment Clause addresses a variety of issues, including prayer in widely varying government settings and financial aid for religious individuals and institutions. "Neutrality has provided a good sense of direction: the government may not favor one religion over another, or religion over irreligion, religious choice being the prerogative of individuals under the Free Exercise Clause" (*McCreary*, 545 U.S. 844, 876). The majority next discussed the intention of the Framers when drafting the religion clauses, arguing that the original intent of the clauses is difficult to discern because of the variety of the views among the Framers.

After *Van Orden v. Perry* (2005) and *McCreary County, Ky. v. ACLU* (2005), it is clear that the Supreme Court now expects a court to look at the full history of a religious display (or other religious act by the state) when determining whether the display (or act) is constitutional. The history was important in both cases. In *Van Orden* the fact that the monument had been on the grounds of the Texas capitol for forty years without incident helped the Court to find the monument constitutional. In *McCreary County* the fact that the counties had recently assembled two more obviously religious displays was the key reason that the court found the displays unconstitutional.

For parents that would attempt to start a religious charter school, the cases have a warning. *McCreary County* informs parents that they cannot draft and redraft the charter making it incrementally less religious in the hopes of creating a charter school as religious as possible. If a court (or a chartering authority) examines a charter to determine whether it is constitutional it will do so in the context of that charter's history.

Additionally, if a charter school, or any public school, creates a religious display, that exhibit will likely be subject to greater scrutiny in light of the statements by many of the Justices that the courts are particularly vigilant when examining church-state issues in elementary and secondary schools. A new display is more likely to be found unconstitutional because it will not have a history of nondivisiveness for a court to look upon. Therefore, if a charter school, or any public school, creates a display it must create one where the context of the display is clearly neutral toward religion and the predominant reason for the display is secular.

Jay v. Freedom From Religion Foundation, Inc. (2007)

The Supreme Court recently heard arguments in *Jay v. Freedom from Religion Foundation, Inc.* This case addresses the issue of standing. Standing relates to when an individual can sue. One of the unique features of the Establishment Clause is that any taxpayer has standing to sue because the use of tax dollars to fund religion is a violation of the Establishment Clause. Standing is very important because without standing an individual cannot file a lawsuit.

In *Jay* (2007) the Supreme Court will address whether taxpayers have standing to challenge the actions of Executive Branch officials pursuant to an Executive Order, rather than an act of Congress. If the Supreme Court narrows standing it will very likely mean that no one will be able to challenge unconstitutional executive actions. However, if the court limits taxpayer standing it may forecast that the current justices of the Supreme Court will be less likely to find any religiously motivated state action unconstitutional.

Jay (2007) is also important because it will be the first Establishment Clause case decided by the current Supreme Court, which includes newly appointed Chief Justice John Roberts and Justice Samuel Alito. *Jay* will be the first opportunity to see how those justices view the Establishment Clause now that they are on the Supreme Court.

RECENT CASES AND CHARTER SCHOOLS

The most recent church-state cases present an unclear picture of the Court's likely decisions regarding religious charter schools. The cases present arguments and support both for the constitutionality and the unconstitutionality of religion-based charter schools. The cases fall into the following categories: state aid cases, public religious activity case, and access cases.

The three aid cases, *Agostini* (1997), *Mitchell* (2000), and *Zelman* (2002), all found funding programs constitutional. These cases, however, do not mean that charter schools would be constitutional as a funding mechanism for religion-based charter schools. Although the reasoning is almost certainly applicable to larger funding issues, all three cases applied to limited or very specific programs. More important, those cases drew a sharp distinction between private-choice aid programs and per-capita aid programs.

Private-choice based aid may flow to religious schools, however, per-capita aid may not. The line between per-capita aid and private-choice aid is not clear from the Court's decisions. Moreover, it is even less clear whether charter schools would be considered one type of program rather than the other. Consequently, the three opinions do not mean that religion-based charter schools are constitutional. However, they are certainly more likely to be found constitutional now than 10 years ago.

The Court examined three religious activity cases, *Santa Fe* (2000), *Van Orden* (2005), and *McCreary County* (2005). *Santa Fe* clearly stands for the proposition that public schools cannot endorse religious activity. Administrators and school boards cannot shift the decision whether to engage in a religious function to students. Moreover, the Court has discounted the argument that religious activities sponsored by a public school can be voluntary. Any religious activity on school grounds must be student-initiated. On the other hand, *Van Orden* and *McCreary County* taken together demonstrate that whether a display of the Ten Commandments is constitutional depends on the history of that display. In the broader sense, those cases provide a warning to parents who would form a religion-based charter school. When examining a charter application, a state reviewing body (and a court) may look at prior applications to determine whether the purpose of the school is to advance religion.

CHAPTER 3

UNDERSTANDING CHARTER SCHOOLS

A Policy Perspective

INTRODUCTION AND OVERVIEW

This chapter examines various policy aspects of charter schools. It first describes the standards on which charter schools are based and how charter schools are structured and then compares these characteristics of charter schools with voucher programs. Next this chapter considers the historical, political, and educational background of charter schools. Even though charter schools are created by state laws, they are really creatures of the political environment and are created and governed by a set of state and local policies that are important to understand in context.

Charter schools address several goals. Raising student achievement and increasing parental involvement are perhaps the two most significant goals that charter schools set out to achieve. Charters realize increased achievement by requiring charter schools to have specific, defined achievement goals that the school operators and founders are bound to accomplish. Charter schools implement parental involvement by shifting some of the power to operate a public school to parents. Law and policy

Religious Charter Schools: Legalities and Practicalites, pp. 59–90
Copyright © 2007 by Information Age Publishing
All rights of reproduction in any form reserved.

are intimately connected with regard to charter schools. Charter schools are defined by state laws to achieve certain policy goals. Additionally, with respect to religion-based charter schools, many potential policy goals are defined or constrained, not only by state charter laws, and constitutions but also by the requirements of the U.S. Constitution.

Charter schools are public schools that operate under different legislated restrictions than other public schools. They are independent public schools that students (really parents) choose to attend but are accountable for results. Charter schools are held accountable through stipulated academic, organizational and financial standards rather than through regulations (Viteritti, 1999, p. 65). Former California Governor Pete Wilson said, "The essential elements of the charter school concept are freedom from state regulation and employee organizational control, and choice on the part of parents, pupils, teachers, and administrators" (Goldstein, 1998, p. 143, citing a letter by the Governor to the State Legislature).

Having primarily addressed the legal context of religion-based charter schools in chapter two, this chapter lays out the why's and how's of charter schools. Next it addresses the historical, political, and educational context of charter schools, including a discussion of the choice movement. Lastly, the hows and whys of charter schools and vouchers are compared because these are the two most politically and legally significant means of educational choice currently being implemented in the United States.

CHARTER SCHOOL STANDARDS

The primary purpose behind charter school policy is defined in terms of student achievement (Cooper, Fusarelli, & Randall, 2004, p. 276). Although educators, policy makers, and legislators, discuss several policy goals of charter schools, it is the question of student achievement that is the driving force behind charter policy and legislation. One principle epitomizes the expectation of all charter schools: "accountability for autonomy" ("Charter Schools," 1998). Accountability is nearly always defined in terms of student achievement, while autonomy is defined through reducing state and district interference.

Enacting charter school legislation has several goals and purposes. Any discussion of the goals of charter schools is usually tied somehow to the goals and purposes of education generally. Lane (1999) uses data compiled by the U.S. Department of Education to summarize those purposes and values:

Charters [do] what public schools already do—just better. Charters [do] something different. Charter schools provide a viable alternative for the "square pegs" in the system. Charter schools provide a testing ground for new governance models [and] innovative teaching strategies. Charter schools can provide choice for all parents and students. Charter schools provide competition to the traditional public school system. Charter schools provide for increased accountability. Charter schools provide for increased accountability in traditional public schools. Charter schools provide the mechanism for organizational changes, allowing opportunity for parents and teachers to teach what they want. Charter schools provide the impetus for system-wide change and reform—a catalyst for change. (p. 3)

These goals can be divided into four categories: (1) implement innovative programs; (2) educate more effectively or efficiently; (3) provide choices; and (4) inspire public schools to be better. Three of four of these goals relate to the general purposes of education. Innovation is necessary to meet changing student needs. The goal of efficiency and effectiveness and the goal of inspiring public schools both relate to educational goals generally in terms of specific (individual charter) and general (public school system) improvement. It is the goal of providing choice, however, that is the most distinct from traditional educational goals. Parental choice in education is a novel political goal; however, it has much support in law.

Charter schools form for two primary reasons: to implement a particular educational vision or to serve a particular student population (Huffman, 1998). Charter schools can implement innovative programs because they are often smaller, more flexible, and lack the bureaucracy of traditional public school systems (Hill, Pierce, & Guthrie, 1997). Surveys of founders and administrators of charter schools illustrate that charter schools form for a variety of additional reasons. Those reasons include educational autonomy, meeting the needs of a specific student population, educational vision, improvement of the teaching and learning environment, instructional innovation, parental involvement, and community partnerships (Kane, 1998; Medler, 1996).

Although a charter school may be larger than an individual district school, the charter school operates as if it were smaller since it is unencumbered by a school district bureaucracy. Unlike most public schools, a charter school is both a school district and a school; consequently, the school is the unit of management and thus can be more efficient and effective (Hill, Pierce, & Guthrie, 1997, p. 56). Additionally, because of the increased accountability, charter schools more overtly exhibit their successes and failures. Accordingly, charter schools are able to implement different methods, curricula, and styles of teaching and governance on a small scale. Theoretically, larger school systems could implement successful aspects or programs used by charter schools.

Accountability for Autonomy

The main justification for exchanging increased autonomy for account-ability is that autonomy will be used to increase student achievement. This can occur for a number of reasons, including the ability of charter schools to implement new or novel programs, charter schools' increased cohesive-ness vis-à-vis public schools, or because charter schools are generally smaller. Andrew Rotherham (1999), in an op-ed piece for *Education Week*, captured the results of charter schools in the title of his article: "When It Comes to School Size, Smaller Is Better" (p. 76).

Charter schools can also provide the "square pegs" of the system with a more appropriate education, often through novel programs, because of the flexibility and attention available in a smaller school without a district bureaucracy. Freeing charter schools from bureaucracy is necessary because bureaucratic systems are inherently resistant to change. Hill, Pierce, and Guthrie (1997) present three kinds of evidence that the cur-rent public school governance system is failing: (1) effective practice in public schools is difficult to reproduce; (2) school systems rarely have available resources to improve failing schools; and (3) the persistence of failure in terms of dropout rates and similar indicators. School autonomy is antithetical to the bureaucratic system and is, therefore, necessary to combat school failure.

One of the reasons for giving charter schools autonomy is to increase parental involvement (Fiske & Ladd, 2000, p. 75). Another is that autonomy is necessary to change instructional and management practices (Hassel, 1999, p. 5, citing Kolderie, 1993). A charter school therefore must be flexible in order to improve.

Choice and Parental Rights

One ever-present argument for charter schools is that choice is inher-ently good. Choice is good because parents, all other things being equal, feel more invested in a school that they have chosen for their children than in a school that has been chosen for them. Moreover, parents are guaranteed by the Constitution some level of choice in their children's education in that they have the right to send their children to a private school. The state, of course, can regulate and supervise all education. However, as the Supreme Court has noted, "The child is not the mere creature of the state; those who nurture him and direct his destiny have the right, coupled with the high duty, to recognize and prepare him for additional obligations" (*Pierce v. Society of Sisters*, 1925, 268 U.S. 510, 536).

Any regulation that interferes with the parents' upbringing of children must be reasonably related to a legitimate state purpose (*Meyer v. Nebraska*, 1923; *Pierce v. Society of Sisters*, 1925, 268 U.S. 510, 536). Thus, parents have the right to choose private or other education for their children. The question becomes whether education is a choice that the state leaves only in the hands of those financially able (Wise, 1968).

For advocates of charter schools from the free market policy perspective, the ultimate objective of any choice initiative is universal choice (Chubb & Moe, 1990; Hill, Pierce, & Guthrie, 1997). In a total choice system, the schools that fail would not be chosen and would therefore close, increasing the overall quality of education. At present, however, charter schools offer a way to improve bad schools by experimenting with new methods of education that can be adopted by failing schools. It is difficult, however, to know whether charter schools will encourage public schools to use their successful methods because of the resistance on the part of district schools to the presence of charter schools (Rosenberg Brigham Assoc., 1998).

Viteritti (1999) connects the vital importance of equality in our society with the goals of charter schools, noting, "A belief in human equality is the foundation of a free society." (p. 23). The principle of equality is of course fundamental to our educational system and is the foundation for this nation's most important legal decision in education, possibly its most important legal decision ever, *Brown v. Board of Education* (1954).

Charter schools, as currently defined, have agreements with the state and exist as a political entity just as school districts do. Regular public schools have no corporate entity. They are wholly subservient to the school districts in which they operate. This is evident through the titles of litigation involving schools. A regular school is accountable to its district, which sets its curriculum, hires its teachers, and sets its policies.

Public schools are accountable to the state in that may lose their accreditation. Charter schools set their own curriculum, hire teachers, and set policies, but those decisions are defined in the charter. If a charter fails to achieve or violates its agreement, it can be closed by the state.

Charter schools and Hill, Pierce, and Guthrie's (1997) contract schools share many principles. Schools should be focused on student learning in a more personalized manner. Schools should be communities that share goals. The school should be the basic unit of management, rather than the school district. Teachers should be treated as professionals. Schools should be equitably funded. Schools should be open to parental participation. Lastly, incentives should encourage high student achievement and efficient use of resources (Hill, Pierce, & Guthrie, pp. 7–10).

Many of these principles, of course, are unrelated to the basic model of charter schools: accountability for autonomy ("Charter Schools," 1998).

Public schools in theory also share a number of these goals: however, charter schools and contract schools are more focused on these particular objectives.

CHARTER SCHOOLS' STRUCTURE

Structurally, charter schools share some qualities of both public and private schools (Finn, Manno, & Vanourek, 2000, pp. 14-15). Like public schools, charter schools are open to all who wish to attend it, without regard to race, religion, academic ability, or ability to pay. Both public and charter schools are held accountable to an authoritative public body (p. 15). Charter schools are different from public schools (depending on the state) in that they can be created by almost anyone, are exempt from many or most state and local public school regulations, are chosen by the families of children who attend, and may be closed if they do not achieve acceptable results. The charter itself is a contract between the school and the public body that authorizes the school (p. 15).

In practice, charters are very similar to what Hill, Pierce, and Guthrie (1997) envision, which is a system where each school contracts with the local school district to operate. The contract would specify the expectations and powers of school, the amount the school would be paid to fulfill those expectations, describe the proposed program and objectives, list the evaluation criteria, and specify the terms for renewal or termination of the contract (p. 133). School districts would hold many contracts with different schools, each with its specific terms and conditions (p. 53).

Contract schools differ from charter schools in one very significant way: charter schools, unlike contract schools, are also school districts. While all aspects of charters do not compare to contract schools, the variety of organizations operating charters is certainly what Hill, Pierce, and Guthrie envisioned.

Charter schools are a relatively recent phenomenon. The first charter school law was passed in Minnesota in 1991 (Minn. Stat. Ann. §1240.10). The "accountability for autonomy" principle dominates the structural dimension of charter schools. Accountability and its assessment are essential to a successful charter program because without assessment there are no means of knowing if an individual charter school is succeeding (Finn, Manno, & Vanourek, 1997).

Ted Kolderie, (1993) noted "nine essentials" that form the core of the charter concept.

1. The school may be organized, owned, and run by any of several parties.
2. The organizers may approach more than one public body for their charter.
3. The school is a legal entity.
4. The school is public (that is nonreligious, does not charge tuition, cannot discriminate or engage in selective admissions, and must follow health and safety laws).
5. The school accepts accountability for the students' academic performance; the school loses its charter if it fails to achieve its goals.
6. The school gets real freedom to change instructional and management practices.
7. The school is a school of choice; no student is required to attend.
8. The state transfers a fair share of school funding from each student's home district to the charter school.
9. Teachers are protected (that is given leaves of absence to teach in charter schools and remain in the retirement system) and given new opportunities to participate in the design of schools.

Although charter standards can be seen behind many of these elements, Kolderie's nine essentials are clearly about how charters are structured. Kolderie's nine essentials are not accepted by all authors and are not evident in all charter systems. However, they do provide a clear overview of the charter concept.

New Zealand implemented a choice system in the 1990s. One aspect of that system was school autonomy. Schools manifested their autonomy in a number of ways including, operational flexibility, opportunities to change struggling schools, and novel academic missions (Fiske & Ladd, 2000, p. 73). Operational flexibility was evident by the ability of principals to use funds more effectively, institute novel programs that involve parents, and to hire teachers that better met the needs of the schools.

Autonomy did not have as significant an effect on parental involvement as had been envisioned by the New Zealand choice system with only 29% of trustees being generally satisfied with parental involvement in their schools. The most striking effects of autonomy were seen in the ability of some principals to use their flexibility to effect "dramatic rescues" of what had been failing schools. Lastly, schools used their autonomy to think about their missions in entirely new ways that varied tremendously.

State Standards

Because state laws define charter schools, their form varies. The characters of individual schools within a state also vary greatly, itself a goal of public charter policy. Moreover, the laws that have been passed are not a "pure" charter program in which all public schools are charters (Hassel, 1998-1, p. 251). Each state's law differs and each law is implemented in a singular fashion.

States vary regarding what entities may authorize charters and determine budgets for charter schools. In Alaska, New Jersey, and many states with charter programs, the state is the only charter-authorizing body and is exclusively responsible for negotiating the basic functions of charter schools, including budgeting and personnel contracts (Center for Education Reform [CER], 2007). Other states, however, allow multiple organizations, such as local school boards, to grant charters (Bierlein, 1997, p 40; CER, 2007). Although the state grants charters in California, that state also requires charters to gain approval by their local school boards (Goldstein, 1998, p. 145).

Charter laws generally have caps on the number of charters that the state will grant, either per year or in total; this number varies greatly from state to state. Arizona, however, does not limit the number of charters that may be granted and as of November 2005 449 charter schools were operating in that state (CER, 2007). A school board, or other governing body of the proposed school, drafts a charter that it proposes to the state. States vary regarding the type of body that may apply for a charter. The state or its designated agent then reviews applications and grants charters up to the cap (maximum number defined by state law). Charters are generally written by schools that seek to be distinctive in some way (Dale, 1997).

Many authors have described ways in which state charter school laws vary. Those characteristics can be divided in the following categories: startup variables, the amount of state support, and the degree of autonomy (Buechler, 1996). Startup variables include the number of schools permitted, variety of sponsors permitted, variety of operators permitted (e.g., school districts, universities, and private entities), variety of schools permitted, existing support required for schools to form, and type of appeals process after denials.

In terms of state support, charter laws vary the structure of the funding process and the amount of start-up funds given by the state. With respect to autonomy, charter statutes vary as to waiver of charter schools from generally applicable regulations, exemption from collective bargaining, amount of legal autonomy, and degree of financial autonomy. In addition to the way that statutes are drafted, states may enforce their charter statutes differently.

The Center for Education Reform defines ten criteria of strong charter laws.

1. Unlimited or substantial number of schools;
2. Multiple chartering authorities;
3. Variety of applicants allowed;
4. Allowing charters to start from non-existing schools;
5. No requirement of formal evidence of local support;
6. Automatic waiver from state regulation;
7. High degree of legal and operational autonomy;
8. Guaranteed full funding;
9. Fiscal autonomy; and
10. Exemption from collective bargaining agreements. (CER, 2004)

States with strong laws (that support charters) on the books may, however, be unexpectedly restrictive in practice. Moreover, the interaction between various characteristics and enforcement creates a great variety of potential charter situations. Massachusetts, for example, has a strong law overall, but originally had a low cap (37, it's now over 100) on the number of chartered schools allowed. Initially the state was the only charter authority in Massachusetts; now local school committees, local teacher unions and the state board of education share charter authority for Horace Mann charter conversions (CER, 2007). There is also evidence that charter schools in states with strong laws have better results (CER, 2004).

The most noteworthy and divisive aspect of charter school legislation is the ability of charter schools in many states to request a waiver from those states' education regulations (Turekian, 1997, p. 1380). The degree to which charter schools are exempt from state regulations varies widely. Arizona and Minnesota provide charter schools with an automatic waiver from most state and district education laws, regulations, and policies (CER, 2007). In Virginia, exemptions are made at the discretion of the school board (CER). In Rhode Island, for a charter school to receive an exemption from district policies, the exemption must be specifically defined in the school's charter (CER).

The arguments for the waiver are that it is necessary to have unconditional autonomy in order to ensure success and that accountability justifies the waiver from state regulations. The waiver from regulations, however, radically changes the nature of the charter school's relationship with the state. The state is not regulating the details of the school; the control is truly on site.

Some authors have argued that the nineteenth-century corporation is the appropriate model for charter schools. The nineteenth-century corporate charter was conceived as a means of the state to subsidize an economic activity that was useful to the public, but which the state did not necessarily feel compelled to undertake itself. Charter schools provide a public good, education. The state shares the educative power with the chartered school because sharing the power benefits the state as a whole, not merely the individuals who have the charter.

Haft (1998) proposes that charter legislation have three elements. First, charter schools should be implemented to achieve statewide educational aims. Second, charter schools should be approved on a case-by-case basis (as they generally are). Third, charter schools should be accountable to the state (p. 1079). Haft's most novel idea is that charter legislation should limit the initial charter applicants to running a single school to maximize the number of varieties of school types. There would be an expectation that successful applicants would later apply to run multiple schools. Haft's model has the benefit that it is different from the modern entity, whether private, public, corporate, or nonprofit. However, Haft ignores parents' significant role in forming the charter schools. The radical change is not merely a different model of a private, public, corporate, or nonprofit entity. The radical change is that the power to form a school is given to the school's clients, the parents. Few parents of successful charter school would consider operating more than one school.

State restrictions on charter law vary widely. These restrictions fine-tune the balance of power between parents and the state, another significant objective of charter policy. In Alaska, teachers at charter schools remain part of the district teachers' union (exemptions can be negotiated) and the charter budget passes through the district. Several other states have the charter budget pass through the district. Another limiting aspect of Alaska's charter system is that charters are only eligible to attend to students in the district where the charter is located.

Connecticut requires that teachers and parents must be represented in the charter school governance system (CER, 2007). Connecticut formally enacts a requirement that charters remain small, they may enroll no more than 250 students for K-8, and no more than 300 or 25% of enrollment in district, whichever is less (CER). Missouri requires that 80% of the full-time teaching staff be certified (CER).

New York previously only allowed 100 new charters to form, but allows an unlimited number for existing schools to convert to charter schools. New York prevents small charters from operating by requiring charter school to enroll 50 students and to employ at least three teachers unless compelling justification is presented. Several states, including Alaska, Connecticut, Massachusetts, and Missouri do not allow for-profit organizations to hold charters, but do not prohibit such organizations from operating them. Lastly, states always have the ability to revoke the charter if accountability standards are not met, which New York did in January 2004 to three schools formed in 1998 (Herszenhorn, 2004).

HISTORICAL CONTEXT

Overview

This book does attempt to review the full history of education in America. It is, however, important to view charter schools in the general context of educational history. This subsection, therefore, provides an overview of some of the important historical periods in American education, focusing on the relationship between religion and the aims of education. First, the chapter examines the nineteenth-century common school movement. The next period focused on is the 1960s through the present. This last discussion focuses on legal history, especially since the 1960s, since most of the changes in public schooling that relate to religion have occurred because of litigation.

Eighteenth and Nineteenth Century American Education

The distinction between the public and private education we know today is very different from colonial times when a "public school" could actually be a private corporation (Jorgenson, 1987, p. 5). The notion of separation between church and state as we know it now had an entirely different meaning: the Establishment Clause protected the religious right of individuals and the states' established religions from interference from the federal government. Public education has been mythologized in society as "a great democratic institution fundamental to America's prosperity and well-being" (Blumenfeld, 1981, p. 1). Arons (1983) explains why it is almost sacrilege to accuse the public schools of ideological censorship.

> Public schooling has so often been regarded as the bulwark of democracy and the nation's chief source of social cohesion and equal opportunity that it may seem subversive to suggest that America's school system has become a suppressor of dissent. (p. 190)

The vision of public schooling as an instrument for social unity, though conceived in the early nineteenth century, resonates today. Most Americans have a remarkably similar vision of what secondary education should be despite the size and diversity of the United States and the politically decentralized character of American schooling (Sizer, 1992, pp. 76–77).

This near uniformity of vision arises from the circle of uniform educational experiences, leading to uniform notions of education, leading to uniform schools, leading to uniform educational experiences, ad infinitum. The uniformity even includes historical falsehoods that are part of our culture (Loewen, 1995). Consequently, compulsory public education has come to mean not only that all citizens are educated, but that, for good or ill, they have nearly uniform educational experiences.

The educational experience of an athletic and an intellectual high school student in the same classes of the same school are going to be radically different (Eckert, 1989; Powell, 1985). There are, however, uniform cultural experiences, which most if not all, public school students share. These cultural experiences include attendance through the nine-month school year, advancing grade by grade, the principal/teacher administrative hierarchy, the recitation of the Pledge of Allegiance, taking standardized tests, and until the 1960s, daily prayer, moments of silence, and Bible readings.

The uniformity of public education is particularly troubling because of the problems caused by the structure of the public school system (Hill, Pierce, & Guthrie, 1997, p. 11). Charter schools are divergent from uniformity because each school is autonomous and can have its own missions and structure (Fiske & Ladd, 2000, p. 73). While school districts are autonomous, individual schools are not. One of the signs that charter schools are nonuniform is that it is so difficult to generalize about charter performance (Finn, Manno, & Vanourek, 2000, p. 77). Charter schools are also encouraged to be different because one of the goals is to offer opportunities for the "square pegs" of the system (Lane, 1999, p. 3).

Notwithstanding this remarkably uniform view of public education, private schools have endured in this country. Nonpublic schooling, however, in Horace Mann's time was chiefly religious, as it is now. Although we currently view public education as necessarily nonreligious, the nineteenth-century vision of the common school was in many ways Protestant (Jorgenson, 1987, pp. 20, 31). For Horace Mann, religious and moral instruction were necessary elements of education (Glenn, 1988, p. 146). Although Mann did not believe in what we would call "separation of church and state," he did assert that only the "common truths" of Christianity should be taught (Jorgenson, p. 20).

All Protestants did not share Mann's view of the "common truths" of Christianity. Mathew Hale Smith accused Mann of disseminating "destructive principles, principles believed to be at war with the Bible" (quoted in Glenn, 1988, p. 187). To Mann, however, the common school religion was not a means of spreading Protestantism. "The primary objective of 'common school religion,' in the minds of Mann and other reformers, was social integration through inculcation of certain common beliefs selected for their presumably uplifting character" (Glenn, 1988, p. 151).

Mann's vision of the importance of education was tied to his views of religion.

> The public highway is not more open and free for every man in the community than is the public schoolhouse for every child; and each parent feels that a free education is as secure a part of the birthright of his offspring as Heaven's bounties of light and air. (Mann, 1846, in Davis, 1979, pp. 42-43)

Mann compared the universal nature of public education to both the mundane (use of highways) and the sacred (Heaven's bounties). Mann ascribes to all parents the belief that a free education is their children's right.

Objections to the religious nature of the common school came from both Orthodox Protestants and from Catholics (Glenn, 1988, pp. 179, 196). Perhaps the most profound objection to the religious nature of the common school was Charles Hodge's.

> What right has the State, a majority of the people, or a mere clique, which in fact commonly control such matters, to say what shall be taught in schools the people sustain? What more right have they to say that no religion be taught, than they have to say that Popery shall be taught? Or what right have the people in one part, to control the wishes and convictions of those in the other part of the State? (Hodge, 1846, quoted in Glenn, p. 183)

Hodge's complaint is not merely religious, but also normative. He opposed the notion of the common school choosing any orthodoxy for all the state's children.

In part to protect their children from exposure to essentially Protestant, and in many instances anti-Catholic, public schools, American Catholics began deliberately forming private schools in the 1840s (Jorgenson, 1987, pp. 72-73). Catholics, however, also objected to theoretically-secular common schools. The nineteenth century Catholic church viewed education as inseparable from religion (Ravitch, 1974, p. 56). Protestants remonstrated against these schools from the 1840s until the late twentieth century.

In 1841, Reverand Lyman Beecher cautioned against the perils of "Popish schools" (Jorgensen, p. 33). This opposition and anti-Catholic bias led Congress in the 1870s to consider and almost pass the Blaine Amendment that would have barred all aid to sectarian (the code word for

Catholic) institutions *Mitchell v. Helms*, 2000, 530 U.S. 793, 828, citing Green, 1992). This biased view of Catholic schools continued until at least 1968 when Justice Black exhibited anti-Catholic bias in his dissent to *Board of Education v. Allen* (1968), which held constitutional the loan of secular textbooks to religious schools.

> The same powerful sectarian religious propagandists who have succeeded in securing passage of the present law to help religious schools carry on their sectarian religious purposes can and doubtless will continue their propaganda, looking toward complete domination and supremacy of their particular brand of religion. (392 U.S. 236, 251, Black, J., dissenting)

Justice Black did not say the word Catholic, but preferred to cite Justice Douglas' dissent, which stated that in Catholic schools textbook choices would be made by, "instructors who are, in the case of Roman Catholic schools, normally priests or nuns" (*Board of Education v. Allen*, 1968, 392 U.S. 236, 255, Douglas, J., dissenting). The *Allen* decision addressed an issue of funding and Black was opposing funding textbook loans to private Catholic schools. However, the notion that Catholics were "looking toward complete domination and supremacy of their particular brand of religion" is offensive and absurd. Ironically he accused Catholics of such an effort to dominate education even as the Unitarian view permeated public schools from the time of the common school (Glenn, 1988, p. 150).

Religion and Public Schools From the 1960s to Today

In the 1960s some parents eventually became disaffected by the generic Protestant trappings of the public school system and used the legal system to remove them. Consequently, the recent history of religion in public schools is a history of court cases. Plaintiffs have successfully argued that Protestant activities in public school violate the Establishment Clause's requirement of nonestablishment of religion. In the 1960s the Court held unconstitutional daily invocations (*Engel v. Vitale*, 1962), daily Bible readings (*Abington v. Schempp*, 1963), and Bible readings and the saying of the Lord's Prayer at school assemblies (*Chamberlin v. Dade County*, 1964).

In the 1970s, the Court turned to examining states' funding private religious schooling. The Court decided almost a dozen of these of cases. During the 1970s, while the courts were addressing the issue of funding private religious education, several educational theorists began putting forth voucher plans (Viteritti, 1999, p. 2). These plans, by authors associated with a liberal social agenda, focused on the educational needs of poor communities with defective education systems.

In the 1980s and 1990s, the Court returned to the issue of religion in public school, holding unconstitutional requiring the posting of the Ten Commandments (*Stone v. Graham*, 1980), daily moments of silence (*Wallace v. Jaffree*, 1985), requiring that creationism be taught along with evolution (*Edwards v. Aguillard*, 1987), and clergy-led prayer at graduation ceremonies (*Lee v. Weisman*, 1992). During the same time period, the Court held constitutional opening state legislatures with prayer (*Marsh v. Chambers*, 1983) and allowing religious groups access to school grounds when other groups are so allowed (*Lamb's Chapel v. Center Moriches*, 1993). The Court has also held that the constitutionality of a religious holiday display depends not on the particular religious symbol, but rather on the context of the display (*Allegheny v. ACLU*, 1989; *Lynch v. Donnelly*, 1984).

Two distinct questions are consistently found in the cases involving religion in a public setting: first, is the intent of the activity is secular or religious; second, does the activity endorse also religion.

Not only must the state refrain from favoring one sect over another, but it also must not favor religion over nonreligion and vice versa. In *Texas Monthly v. Bullock* (1989) the Court held unconstitutional a tax-exemption for religious periodicals. Writing in concurrence, Justice Blackmun, joined by Justice O'Connor, noted that the tax-exemption did not apply to philosophical literature distributed by nonreligious organizations. Thus, the statute favored religion over nonreligion. The Court has refused to differentiate between nonsectarian prayer and sectarian prayer.

The opinions striking down the various religious activities that the state imposed on public schools are anything but antagonistic to religion. Justice Kennedy wrote, "We express no hostility to [religious] aspirations, nor would our oath permit us to do so" (*Lee v. Weisman*, 1992, 505 U.S. 577, 598). Neutrality means that the state may neither advance nor inhibit religion.

As discussed in chapter two, the Supreme Court has sometimes seemed to interpret the Establishment Clause differently for schools when compared with other institutions.

The Court has been particularly vigilant in monitoring compliance with the Establishment Clause in elementary and secondary schools. Families entrust public schools with the education of their children, but condition their trust on the understanding that the classroom will not purposely be used to advance religious views that may conflict with the private beliefs of the student and his or her family. Students in such institutions are impressionable and their attendance is involuntary. (*Edwards v. Aguillard*, 1987, 482 U.S. 578, 583-84)

Unfortunately, the issue of the appropriate place of religion in schools today is far from settled.

Administrators appear on both sides of the issue. At least one principal has removed the Bible from a school library on the grounds that she thought the Establishment Clause required her to remove it (*Roberts v. Madigan*, 1990). At another school, the administration encouraged student-led prayer in order to circumnavigate restrictions against school sponsored prayer (*Chandler v. James*, 1997). Moreover, parents are becoming increasingly uncomfortable with school activities that are either religious or that offend their religious beliefs.

In *Altman v. Bedford Central School District* (1999), parents sued arguing that several school activities violated the First Amendment. The activities were diverse and the New York District Court reached varying conclusions about the activities' constitutionality. The conclusions included the following: constructing the likeness of a Hindu deity (unconstitutional), school sponsorship of "worry dolls" (unconstitutional), lectures on rocks and minerals (constitutional), Drug Abuse Resistance Education (constitutional), Yoga exercises (constitutional), a "Magic: The Gathering" student club (constitutional), and reading lessons about Buddha and Quezalcoatl (constitutional).

Whether an activity is constitutional or unconstitutional is not as important to parents as the breadth of those activities. Parents are becoming increasingly uncomfortable with activities that their children are required to perform or learn in school. Students must be exempted from any overt act that violates their religious beliefs (*West Virginia v. Barnette*, 1943). Students, however, are not entitled to an exemption if they are merely learning information contrary to their religious beliefs (*Mozert v. Hawkins County Board of Education*, 1987).

Mozert (1987), discussed in chapter one, involved fundamentalist Christians who found various readings in the school reader objectionable; this included discussions of Chinese, Islamic, and Buddhist philosophy. Parents objected to their children learning about other religions. That objection is not protected by law. Nor are parents entitled to an exemption if they merely find the activities repugnant (*Herndon v. Chapel-Hill*, 1996). The activity must violate the religious belief. Parental conflicts with administrators over books are also increasing (Arons, 1983, p. 14). As parents, particularly religious parents, become disaffected by public schools, it is likely that they will turn increasingly to charter schools instead of litigation as it becomes settled law that their children are not entitled to exemptions from many activities that they find repugnant.

THE POLITICAL CONTEXT

Political Dynamics

As with most proposals to change educational governance, legislation enacting charter schools has not occurred without struggle in state legislatures (Viteritti, 1999, p. 69). Education laws are often passed for political reasons and charter laws are no exception; therefore, charter laws mix law and policy. Charter legislation, along with other choice proposals, has generated "vicious rhetoric" and "outright hostility" (Fusarelli, 2003, p. 1).

Local school boards have not voluntarily given up power, students, and money (Viteritti, 1999, p. 69). Teachers unions have also opposed charters primarily because of charters' ability to negotiate contracts outside of collective bargaining agreements (Viteritti, p. 69). Thus, those working for charter school reform had the benefits and burdens of previous battles over choice.

Often these battles over school choice are affected by the institutional structure of governance in the United States (Fusarelli, 2003, p. 46). State constitutions often create the conditions that determine the forms of choice enacted in a state, creating what the Center for Education Reform refers to as a strong or weak charter law (2007). Another key institutional factor is the length of a state's legislative session; Texas happens to have a particularly short one, which affected how its charter law was lobbied and passed (Fusarelli, 2003). A state constitutional provision or legislative act is often not the last word, with both proponents and opponents of choice using litigation to achieve their goals vis-à-vis choice.

Although the institutions are of course important when enacting a choice proposal, it is often the policymakers, activists, and interest groups that determine the outcome of a policy initiative (Fusarelli, 2003, p. 71). Texas was unable to pass a voucher law, but did pass a charter statute. After a lengthy analysis of voucher coalitions, Fusarelli discusses charter schools, noting, "What is most remarkable about the politics surrounding charter schools in Texas and in many other states is how little opposition has arisen to various charter proposals, in comparison to vouchers" (p. 90). Several persons and groups that had worked against voucher proposals supported charter proposals, including the Texas PTA.

Charters were viewed by some a compromise, giving parents choices without diverting public funds to private schools. The Texas Federation of Teachers stated that it would support charter proposals so long as they were organized by teachers or in conjunction with teachers (Fusarelli, 2003, p. 90). The law in place at present defines eligible applicants as parents and teachers at existing public schools for conversion charters and in open-enrollment charters, as existing public or private schools, parents, teachers, public or private institutions of higher education, non-profit organizations, governmental entities.

Fusarelli (2003) concludes that the Texas charter law was enacted for two reasons. First, charter schools had support in the legislature and executive on a bipartisan basis. Second, the opposition to charters did not unite into a coherent opposition group because the charter proposal did not generate as much enmity as the voucher proposals.

Public support for school choice has gradually increased since 1994 (Fusarelli, 2003, p. 3). One of the notable distinctions in public attitudes toward choice proposals is that those who are more likely to have been failed by the current education system are more likely to support choice proposals: blacks and Hispanics favor choice more than whites; the poor support choice more than the middle class; and urban dwellers back choice more than suburbanites (Fusarelli, p. 5; Viteritti, 1999, p. 5-7).

Given that the nation's urban schools are failing ("Quality Counts," 1998, p. 12), it is not surprising that the two most famous voucher programs in the nation (and the first to include religion-based schools) are in Milwaukee and Cleveland. A comparison of the large number of charter laws enacted across the nation and the handful of voucher programs illustrates the incredible political success that charter proponents have had when compared with voucher advocacy groups.

The Choice Movement

Charter school legislation is one example of the general movement across the country toward school choice. The modern school choice movement is traced to a 1955 essay by Milton Friedman (Viteritti, 1999, p. 2, citing Friedman, 1955). Although school choice is often categorized as new, recent, or untried, Vermont has the longest running school choice program in the nation. In Vermont, the state pays tuition expenses for children attending any school, including nonsectarian private ones if the local town has no school. Although support for vouchers has grown slowly, public support for school choice has increased in recent years.

School choice includes other methods of reform such as tuition tax credits, vouchers, and privatization. The issue of school choice, however, has become so complex that one form of choice competes with another (e.g., vouchers versus charter schools) (Morken & Formicola, 1999, p. 58). Evangelicals, for example, fought the passing of charter school laws in Colorado, favoring tax-credits; however, once the charter law was passed, Evangelicals flocked to charter schools (Morken & Formicola, p. 57).

School choice is said to have various beneficial outcomes, including lessening bureaucracy and increasing accountability and performance. Other arguments for choice include the need for increasing fairness between social classes and increasing parental rights in education (Bolick, 1998; Chubb & Moe, 1990; Coons, 1989; Glenn, 1998; Viteritti, 1999). The common feature of all choice programs is that they increase educational opportunity.

There are several ways that school choice can operate. Methods of school choice, from the least to the most expansive, include intradistrict choice (allowing students to attend any school in his or her home district), magnet schools (allowing some schools in a district to cultivate an identity and attract students from the entire district), charter schools (allowing some schools to in the state to cultivate an identity and avoid many state regulations), interdistrict choice (allowing students to attend any public school in the state), and vouchers (giving a defined group of students a negotiable claim to public funding that can be redeemed at schools in lieu of tuition).

Often interdistrict or intradistrict choice methods do not allow free movement between or within school districts. Such systems often are tied to desegregation and achieving racial balances in schools. The same is often true for magnet schools. These choices are all in addition to the informal, but important, "choice" of parents to choose their residence based on the quality of a school district; this choice is nearly always directly related to parents' economic capacity (Wise, 1968).

Each method of choice has its supporters and detractors, and charter schools are no exception. Some advocates of charter schools view them as a compromise because a true choice system (i.e., a universal voucher system) is not viable. The most common comparison made between choice alternatives is between charters and vouchers. Vouchers and charters, however, are more than two means of implementing choice. Vouchers allow parents to choose between public and private entities. Charters allow parents to create a public entity.

The Market Metaphor

An important aspect of the choice movement is the application of a market metaphor to education. The market (supply and demand) is used to advocate school choice because a choice of schools increases demand for higher quality products (better education) (Friedman, 1955). Finn, Manno, and Vanourek (2000) compare the problem of a universal public school system with little competition to the U.S. Postal Service before the advent of Federal Express. According to the argument, poor quality sellers (bad schools) will go out of business and high quality sellers (good schools) will expand and thrive (increase enrollment). According to the market metaphor, autonomy enables schools to innovate and to adapt (Haft, 1998).

While this metaphor has been used by other authors, the most detailed argument utilizing the market metaphor was made by Chubb and Moe (1990) in *Politics Markets and America's Schools*. Chubb and Moe argue that the basic bureaucratic structure of our public school system is the root of our educational problems. Although their work was one in a long line of surveys that compared the success of public and private schools, Chubb and Moe notably used that research to frankly analyze educational institutions.

Chubb and Moe (1990) argue that to solve the problems we need a new governance structure. All other solutions are merely attempt to impose desirable characteristics (e.g., high standards) on schools and are only temporary patches on a defective system. Chubb and Moe propose to look beyond the public school system and to alternative institutional arrangements. A universal charter school system would change the structure of the school governance system by fusing the school and the school district.

Fairness

Another strong argument in favor of choice is fairness. "To achieve educational and social equality in the United States, we need to empower poor parents to act in the best interests of their children and offer them alternatives to failing schools" (Viteritti, 1999, p. vii). The rich, unlike the poor, can choose schools by choosing where they live or by paying for private schools (Wise, 1968). According to the National Center for Education Statistics 60% parents with children in public schools with incomes of $50,000 or more said that school quality was a factor in choosing residence. Whereas only 40% of those with an income of $15,000 or less cited school quality as a factor choosing residence (Viteritti, 1991, p. 11, citing National Center for Education Statistics, "National Household Education Survey," *The Condition of Education*, 1997).

Of course, the residential choices available to a parent making $15,000 annually are very different from those available to one making $50,000 (Ehrenreich, 2001). The school choice movement is one means of alleviating this disparity. One argument against choice is that allowing some students to attend charter schools (or giving some students vouchers) increases educational inequality. The two counter arguments are that this inequality would not exist in a universal charter (or voucher) system and that a partial charter (or voucher) system at least gives some poor students the educational opportunities of the rich.

Objections to Choice Proposals

The major objection to choice proposals is that the market metaphor is inappropriate for education. Some authors argue that the market metaphor used by advocates of choice is wholly inappropriate. "There are important ways in which education is not like haircuts, or cars, or other material goods that are privately purchased and consumed" (Henig, 1994, p. 58). Objections to the market metaphor stem from the unquantifiable nature of the "educational product." Opponents also maintain that private providers may not properly balance social and individual interests; since enforcement of performance may be difficult, private providers in education would require constant monitoring. Ultimately, public education may not be amenable to profit.

Opponents of choice maintain that what is needed is not choice, but rather reform of the system. Other authors argue that it was the market that altered the character of individual districts and shaped schools that caused many of the problems in education; consequently, giving more power to the education market would make things worse (Weeres, 1990). Another argument against choice is that the Constitution requires the state to prevent religious groups from forming schools (Dwyer, 1998).

Three of the weaknesses of antichoice arguments are obvious. First, a market in education does not necessarily mean there will be for-profit schools. In fact, most private schools are operated by nonprofit organizations. Second, the argument that the Constitution prohibits religious groups from forming such schools is not entirely clear; even if such religious schools were absolutely banned, it does not present a valid argument against choice generally, merely for excluding unconstitutional schools. Third, while the contention that the educational product is difficult to quantify is straightforward, the standards and testing movements, codified by the No Child Left Behind, undermine this contention.

The argument that choice may lead to social stratification and a situation where the White and middle-class students attend the best schools while the poor and Black students attend failing ones is not far from the present situation (Viteritti, 1999, p. 13). The arguments against choice are not sufficient to oppose charter schools because charter schools as a means of school reform are more than a method of choice. Charter schools also serve the goals of innovation, efficiency, and serving specific student populations.

Arguments for Charter Schools

Hill, Guthrie, and Pierce's (1997) strongest argument in favor of contract schools, which are similar in structure to charter schools, is that the school should be the basic unit of management (pp. 8, 56–57). Under the current system most management occurs at the district level. The form of district school systems (as opposed to individual schools) creates several obstacles to effective education.

Schools are often more concerned with fulfilling government mandates than community needs; parents feel disaffected by their complete removal from the decision-making process; and schools make defensive decisions to avoid legal consequences rather than focusing on the needs of actual students (Hill, Guthrie, & Pierce's, pp. 31–32). Thus, each school within a larger district must meet the common political needs of the entire district even though, as a consequence, the individual schools may not meet the needs of their respective communities.

All of these problems are exacerbated by the organization of central offices where multiple assistant-superintendents have independent yet overlapping spheres of influence. Public schools have created this problem by growing as a monopoly, eliminating reasons to function efficiently (Peterson, 1990).

THE EDUCATIONAL CONTEXT

A Nation at Risk, Public Schools, and Charter Schools

In 1984 the National Commission on Excellence in Education published *A Nation At Risk*, beginning an era of panic, frustration, and educational reform. Its second chapter states the problem.

> Our Nation is at risk. Our once unchallenged preeminence in commerce, industry, science, and technological innovation is being overtaken by competitors throughout the world.... We report to the American people that while we take justifiable pride in what our schools and colleges have historically accomplished and contributed to the Unites States and the well-being of its people, the educational foundations of our society are presently being eroded by a rising tide of mediocrity that threatens our very future as a Nation and a people. (1984/1994, p. 5)

Since the publication of *A Nation at Risk*, educational reformers have proposed various means of combating the "rising tide of mediocrity."

Unfortunately, current educational research, rather than focusing on the school as a whole, usually examines discrete components such as instructional methods and means of funding (Hill, Pierce, & Guthrie, 1997, pp. 56–57). Those reforms have filled the spectrum from the sublime, creating schools based on character education (Kilpatrick, 1992; Wynne & Ryan, 1997), to the ridiculous, posting the Ten Commandments in schools (Walsh, 1999). The litany of reforms includes charter schools. Charter schools, however, unlike other reforms, challenge the very notion of what it means to be a "public school."

A public or common school was defined by a Massachusetts court in 1866 "as a school (1) 'supported by general taxation,' (2) 'open to all free of expense,' and (3) 'under the immediate control and superintendence of agents appointed by the voters of each town and city' " (Jorgenson, 1987, p. 7). Charter schools fit the first two of those categories. Charter schools are public schools that are different from traditional public schools in a number of ways.

Statutes authorizing charter schools encourage schools that are more concerned with parental involvement; at a minimum parents are involved by choosing the school. Charter schools are theoretically supposed to improve performance by eliminating regulations rather than by using regulations to monitor or ensure performance. Lastly, charter schools aim to be different from one another by avoiding the cookie cutter rationalization of school-district uniformity. Enacting charter school legislation creates "separation between school and state" (Arons, 1983, p. 213).

Charter schools create a buffer that prevents the state from imposing a universal ideology, such as the original common schools did, upon students. The state is not only allowing private schools to function independently, but also is retreating from its active involvement in schooling. Although the state should ensure a high quality of education, it is doubtful that the state must provide the education itself.

The radical change proposed by charter schools has its roots in the problems caused by the uniformity of public schools. Charter schools rest on a "devastating critique of the present system because it implies that for a school meaningfully to innovate ... it must be free of the usual rules, regulations, and traditions of a school system" (Sarason, 1998, p. 18). Consequently, charter schools are meant to be a vehicle for creating public schools that are freer to innovate. Charter schools enable the state to create public schools without traditional bureaucracy and test whether their educational output meaningfully improves. Moreover, parents share the power to create a public school with the state.

As the founder of one California charter school said, "This charter school law is my license to dream, to do what I have always known needed to be done for my kids, but was not doable because of the system, too many excuses, and a lack of accountability" (quoted in Bierlein, 1997, p. 37). The common perception found in Colorado, however, was that parents should be held accountable for failing students more than public schools (Morken & Formicola, 1999, p. 50). This sentiment is often translated into contempt for the poor rather than concern for their schools.

What is a Public School?

Public education has become America's most common cultural experience and its biggest business (Arons, 1983, p. 88). Public schools have also become a major battleground in the culture wars (Graff, 1992). "It is because of the intrinsic link between public education, community and national identity, and the future (symbolized by children) that the institutions of education have long been a political and legal battleground" (Hunter, 1991, p. 198). These battles often find their basis in religious beliefs and in conflicting notions of what is best for students. In the 1920s, for example, the move toward statutes banning the teaching of evolution was based on the idea that such teaching was bad for students' souls (Larson, 1989, p. 44).

In *Brown v. Board of Education* (1954) the Supreme Court, speaking unanimously, noted, "Today, education is perhaps the most important function of state and local governments" (347 U.S. 483, 493). Elaborating upon this the Court added:

> Compulsory school attendance laws and the great expenditures for education both demonstrate our recognition of the importance of education to our democratic society. It is required in the performance of our most basic public responsibilities, even service in the armed forces. It is the very foundation of good citizenship. Today it is a principal instrument in awakening the child to cultural values, in preparing him for later professional training, and in helping him to adjust normally to his environment. In these days, it is doubtful that any child may reasonably be expected to succeed in life if he is denied the opportunity of an education. Such an opportunity, where the state has undertaken to provide it, is a right which must be made available to all on equal terms. (347 U.S. 483, 493)

Although the Court notes the importance of public education to society, the opinion notes that public education is a right only "where the state has undertaken it."

Public education is not a fundamental right (*Plyler v. Doe*, 1982). Moreover, much of the reasoning rests not on the importance of public education, but of education itself in achieving full partnership in American society.

The Court had previously held that although the states could regulate public and private schools they could not ban private schools (*Pierce v.*

Society of Sisters, 1925), regulate private schools out of existence (*Farrington v. Tokushige*, 1927), or excessively limit aspects of private schools' curricula (*Meyer v. Nebraska*, 1923). Consequently, even the most important Supreme Court opinion in the realm of public education, *Brown v. Board of Education* (1954) speaks primarily of the importance of education to the state rather than the importance of *public* education to the state. An educated populace is the policy goal, not a populace uniformly educated by the state.

Conflicting Rights and Education

Parents and the state often have conflicting interests in education. It is only in rare instances that parents' interests are so important that the Constitution requires that the parents' interest trumps the state's. Charter schools tinker with that dynamic and shift the balance toward the parent vis-à-vis the state with regard to education.

The Supreme Court, in *West Virginia v. Barnette* (1943) noted, "If there is any fixed star in our constitutional constellation, it is that no official, high or petty, can prescribe what shall be orthodox in politics, nationalism, religion, or other matters of opinion" (319 U.S. 624, 642). The Court held that it was unconstitutional for the state to force Jehovah's Witnesses schoolchildren to pledge allegiance to the American Flag in violation of their religion. The state cannot, without a compelling reason, require students to perform an act that violates their religious beliefs.

Courts, however, have been less sympathetic to parents who want their children to avoid learning about topics that violate their religious beliefs. As discussed in chapter one, *Mozert v. Hawkins* (1987) held that fundamentalist Christian parents had no right to prevent their children from being exposed to information about other religions or lessons that violated their beliefs, such as lessons about evolution.

If parents want their children to avoid learning about activities that violate their religious beliefs, they have had two options: private school or home schooling. Even then, however, the state still has the potential to exact tremendous influence over their children's education. Although the state cannot excessively regulate private schools (*Farrington v. Tokushige*, 1927), the state may impose any reasonable regulations (*Pierce v. Society of Sisters*, 1925). Similarly, the state may impose reasonable regulations and limitations on home schooling including, for example, state-administered achievement tests (*Murphy v. Arkansas*, 1988) or banning home-schooled students from attending public school part-time (*Swanson v. Guthrie*, 1998).

One notable exception to the many cases in which the state curriculum trumps parental rights is the Old Order Amish. In *Wisconsin v. Yoder* (1972), the Supreme Court held that the unique nature of Amish society prevented the state from compelling students to attend conventional school beyond age 14.

The Court held that this right of exemption from compulsory schooling between ages 14 and 16 arose from two sources: parental rights and the right to free exercise of religion.

> The Court [has acknowledged] the rights of parents to direct the religious upbringing of their children. And, when the interests of parenthood are combined with a free exercise claim of the nature revealed by this record, more than merely a "reasonable relation to some purpose within the competency of the State" is required to sustain the validity of the State's requirement under the First Amendment. (*Wisconsin v. Yoder*, 1972, 406 U.S. 205, 233)

Directing religious upbringing, however, has in most instances, not been enough to require the state to grant an exemption from activities on religious grounds (*Swanson v. Guthrie*, 1998; *Murphy v. Arkansas*, 1988).

The various courts rulings make sense in many ways. Requiring a student to commit an act that violates her religion is fundamentally different from requiring her to learn about something that disagrees with her religion. Additionally, exemptions from subject matter, though important to parents, would make things much more difficult for the school and teacher, especially if exemptions proliferated. Consequently, it becomes easier for the school or teacher to omit objectionable material than to create multiple lessons.

Moreover, it is reasonable that any exemption must be based on high stakes. The old order Amish society successfully argued that it was threatened with destruction by the compulsory education program. Few parents could similarly argue that learning material contrary to their beliefs would destroy their religion.

Two problems are evident from this line of cases. First, it seems unfair that a religion must be threatened with extinction before students can opt-out of religiously offensive material. Second, a uniform orthodoxy within public education is antithetical to the Supreme Court's warning that "it is a central tenet of the First Amendment that the government must remain neutral in the marketplace of ideas" (*FCC v. Pacifica Foundation*, 1978, 438 U.S. 726, 746).

In recognizing a constitutional exemption from saluting the flag by the Jehovah's Witnesses, the Court described the lengths the state took to force the children to salute the flag (*West Virginia v. Barnette*, 1943). Parents were willing to go to such lengths, risking jail, to prevent their children from violating their religious beliefs and pledging allegiance to the flag.

Similarly, Vicky Frost allowed herself to be arrested while protesting the school board's refusal to exempt her child from stories she found religiously objectionable (*Frost v. Hawkins County Board of Education*, 1988). To be sure, parents have the option to send their children to private schools. But, it is unreasonable to expect parents who find lessons objectionable to send their children to private schools for two reasons. First, private schools can be unduly expensive. Second, public schools are supposed to serve the entire community.

By choosing a singular worldview, whether it is the nondenominational Protestantism of the nineteenth century, or the supposed secular humanism of the late twentieth century, public education is defining orthodoxy. Free education comes with a price, but the Supreme Court has noted that this country was not founded on uniformity, but rather on pluralism.

> We can have intellectual individualism and the rich cultural diversities that we owe to exceptional minds only at the price of occasional eccentricity and abnormal attitudes. When they are so harmless to others or to the State as those we deal with here, the price is not too great. But freedom to differ is not limited to things that do not matter much. That would be a mere shadow of freedom. The test of its substance is the right to differ as to things that touch the heart of the existing order. (*West Virginia v. Barnette*, 1943, 319 U.S. 624, 641)

The state's interest in education has many dimensions, but perhaps the most important is fostering political participation by citizens. Participation in the political process increases with one's education (Viteritti, 1999, p. 180). Courts have generally given great deference states in their role as educators. The standard of scrutiny for alleged infringements of educational rights is one of reasonableness, the lowest level of protection given to constitutional rights (*Pierce v. Society of Sisters*, 1925).

The use of this standard does not devalue the rights of parents, but rather illustrates the state's compelling interest in an educated populace and the Supreme Court's view that the right to education has only limited constitutional protection (*San Antonio v. Rodriguez*, 1973). Consequently, the courts have allowed school administrators to exercise tremendous control over the curriculum (*Bethel School Dist. v. Fraser*, 1986).

Moreover, in cases involving funding private religious education, the Supreme Court has consistently held that such funding has a permissible public purpose, even when it may have the unconstitutional effect of advancing religion. "A State always has a legitimate concern for maintaining minimum standards in *all* schools it allows to operate" (*Lemon v. Kurtzman*, 1971, 403 U.S. 602, 613). The state's interest in education is so great that it would be irrational (and unconstitutional) for it to deny education to the children of illegal immigrants (*Plyler v. Doe*, 1982).

Parents' rights to educate their children and the state's right to educate its populace must be balanced. It is only when some additional right is implicated that the balance tips to one or the other. In many instances, however, the right of the state and the rights of parents balance equally, yet one side wins and another loses. These choices must be fundamental choices of principle (Tribe, 1985, p. viii). The principle crafted by the courts has been that if students are required to perform an action or affirmation, the parents win, but if students are forced to learn a lesson, the school wins.

States, however, do not have to draw the line there. States may give more rights to parents than the constitution requires. Charter schools are an effort by the states to do just that. They not only give parents the right to choose a school, but also give parents the right to create a school. This is a fundamental shift in the balance between parents and the states.

COMPARING CHARTERS AND VOUCHERS

In a voucher system, parents are given a voucher they can use to pay for all or part of their child's education. In the Cleveland voucher program, parents, defined by income level, were given vouchers that they could use to pay for all educational expenses at public schools in school districts adjacent to Cleveland or make partial payment at private schools located in the Cleveland District (*Zelman v. Simmons-Harris*, 2002).

One similarity between the way charters and vouchers are funded is that the state gives the school money on a per pupil basis. The school keeps receiving funding only so long as it produces satisfactory results (which are more rigidly defined in charter systems) and the child attends the school.

Five arguments are put forth that charters are actually preferable to vouchers: (1) charter schools may not have admissions standards; (2) charter schools may not charge tuition; (3) charter schools must obtain authorization from the state; (4) charter schools must meet performance contracts or close; and (5) charter schools may not be religious (Hassel, 1998, pp. 35-37).

These arguments ignore the fact, however, that a charter system could be designed without standards, allow tuition, and so forth; while a vouchers strategy could be designed in which schools are held accountable to state standards, participating students cannot be charged tuition, or participating schools must be nonreligious. For example, the state could prohibit schools that receive vouchers from using admission standards or from charging voucher students additional tuition beyond the voucher. The Cleveland voucher program limited the students' copayment to $250. The state could also require private schools that receive vouchers to obtain authorization and meet performance standards. Moreover, most states with voucher programs still exclude religious schools.

The difference between charter and voucher systems is not in these kinds of details, but rather in how the choice system is *implemented*. Vouchers implement choice by giving parents money (in the form of a voucher) to choose among private and out-of-district schools. Charters implement choice by creating free schools to which parents can send their children. The legal distinction between these programs becomes clear reading Justice O'Connor's concurrence in *Mitchell v. Helms* (2000):

> I do not believe that we should treat a per-capita-aid program the same as the true private-choice programs.... First, when the government provides aid directly to the student beneficiary, that student can attend a religious school and yet retain control over whether the secular government aid will be applied toward the religious education. The fact that aid flows to the religious school and is used for the advancement of religion is therefore wholly dependent on the student's private decision. (530 U.S. 793, 842)

Charter schools may be a per-capita aid program because the school receives funds directly from the state on a per-pupil basis and those funds are not earmarked toward a specific educational program, as was the case in *Mitchell*; however, it is unclear whether charters might instead be considered a private choice program.

Another difference between voucher programs and charter schools is the possibility of schools similarly situated (having the same regulatory status) that are not part of the educational funding program. In a voucher program, private schools can choose not to accept vouchers. A private school could be made up of a mix of students that use and do not use the voucher. Such was the situation in the Cleveland voucher program. Charter schools, however, by definition are all funded similarly and have the same regulatory status within a state. The state could not constitutionally require all private schools to meet the standards of voucher recipients, but the state has broad authority to attach strings to funds (*South Dakota v. Dole*, 1987).

Charter school legislation allows parents to create public schools that fit their needs. Charter schools give parents the authority to operate a public school, not merely money to attend a private one. Consequently, the function of public schools has changed. The parent is no longer expected to want the same thing for his child as the community (Dewey, 1900/1969, p. 7). By creating charter schools the state assists that parental duty rather than co-opting that duty and assuming that both the parent and the state want the same thing for the child.

As discussed in the previous chapter, the concurrence in *Mitchell v. Helms* (2000) makes a distinction between aid programs that benefit faith-based organizations. "[P]er-capita-aid program[s]" are unconstitutional, while "true private-choice programs" are constitutional. In her concurring opinion Justice O'Connor noted,

> [W]hen the government provides aid directly to the student beneficiary, that student can attend a religious school and yet retain control over whether the secular government aid will be applied toward the religious education. The fact that aid flows to the religious school and is used for the advancement of religion is therefore wholly dependent on the student's private decision. (530 U.S. 793, 842)

The Supreme Court used the *Mitchell* concurrence to hold the Cleveland voucher program constitutional because it was a true private-choice program (*Zelman v. Simmons-Harris*, 2002). Although the Cleveland voucher program was specifically targeted to poor students, there is nothing in the opinion that limits its holding to such programs.

The key elements of the Cleveland voucher program that made it constitutional were that the voucher recipients were not defined on the basis of religion and that the recipients could choose any school, without any preference given to private or faith-based schools. Therefore, the constitutional impediment to a universal voucher system has been mostly, if not entirely, eliminated by recent Supreme Court decisions.

Charters, on the other hand, present a different legal issue for two reasons. First, charter schools are very probably state actors; therefore, the constitutionality of religion-based charters is not merely a funding issue. Second, even if charter schools are not state actors, because they are structurally different from vouchers, the recent Supreme Court decisions do not mean that religion-based charters are constitutional. The aid goes to a charter on a per-capita basis, not directly to the student beneficiary.

Although the per-capita aid flows to the charter on the basis of a students' (or her parents') choice to attend the school, the *Mitchell* (2000) concurrence would probably define charter schools an unconstitutional per-capita program rather than a constitutional private-choice program. If families got a check they could use at any charter school then the legal issue would be entirely different and the voucher standard set by the Supreme Court would probably settle the issue. Perhaps it is this legal distinction that makes charter school systems more politically palatable than voucher programs (Fusarelli, 2003).

CONCLUSION

State statutes creating charter schools are redefining the meaning of public schooling. Charter schools attempt to resolve the educational crisis in ways that are compatible with democratic values. Although the notion of what constitutes the curriculum and format of public schools has changed through the past 170 years, one thing had not—the notion that public education should be uniform. Indeed, much in the recent reform agenda, particularly the standards movement, presses for greater uniformity.

Currently, various authors argue that public education should be nonuniform (Viteritti, 1999) or that education would benefit from market-type competition for students (Chubb & Moe, 1990). Charter schools address this new trend in two ways. First, by their very nature, charter schools are nonuniform. Disparate groups, whose needs aren't being met by public schools, often form charter schools. Second, charter schools are a means for creating competition within the public schools since they are funded based on the number of students who choose them.

Such competition is a direct utilization of market theory applied to education. Charter schools also help guard against the state using public schools to indoctrinate its students. "The best guarantee against institutional indoctrination is that there be a plurality or institutions (Thiessen, 1993, p. 274). Charter schools, however, are more than market theory, more than educational choice, and more than a means of creating different types of educational institutions: they are a radical new way of looking at what it means to be a "public" school.

One of the reasons Horace Mann offered when promoting the common school idea was the potential social and political crisis if the next generation was not molded into his vision of American values (Glenn, 1988, p. 63). The common school was needed to shape society because Mann and his followers held a pessimistic view of the future of American society. This was based on fear of the changes caused by immigration, urbanization and Catholicism (Glenn, pp. 63–68). Because of these fears, Man did not want to leave popular education to private organizations.

James Carter, in his *Essays on Popular Education* wrote, "Every private establishment detaches a portion of the community from the great mass, and weakens or destroys their interest in those means of education which are common to the whole people" (quoted in Glenn, 1988, p. 75). Consequently, the monopoly of public education was in theory necessary for the good of the country.

These early nineteenth-century opinions of private education have not survived through time. The Supreme Court has stated that private education is useful and meritorious (*Pierce v. Society of Sisters*, 1925). During the 2000 campaign, George W. Bush in fact proposed that poor parents who send their children to Title I schools that perform unsuccessfully be entitled to a voucher in the amount of their child's Title I funds; parents could use this voucher to send their child to a private school (Johnston, 1999). This plan of course did not survive the compromise bill that passed in Congress, which did not include any voucher provision (McCaleb, 2001).

Charter schools are in many ways a return to the nineteenth-century model of a public school. They are community centered and nonbureaucratic. However, charter schools have some of the same problems that nineteenth-century schools had. The problems of those schools were Protestantism and narrowness. Charter schools have a tremendous opportunity to be accommodating to religious parents; however, the law does not allow charters as public schools to be religiously indoctrinating or even endorsing.

The ones now clamoring for change are often religious Protestants (Morken & Formicola, 1999, p. 57). Religious Protestants became disaffected with the public school system after the removal of prayers and other religious activities and artifacts; it is often those religious Protestant parents who have sued arguing that public schools violate their rights to raise their children religiously (*Mozert v. Hawkins*, 1987; Somerville, 2001).

In 1975 home schooling was illegal and often criminalized in almost all fifty states. By 1993 that situation had changed with all states allowing home schooling; proponents of home schooling, who were very often Fundamentalist Christians, accomplished this through court challenges and lobbying efforts nationwide (Somerville, 2001). That home schooling is no longer illegal is certainly a good thing.

Charter schools, however, are unlike home schooling. A parent who home schools can use those lessons to indoctrinate her children into her faith. Religious parents who start a charter school, however, cannot. Charter schools can only be a vehicle for religious parents to provide their children with a secular education. Charter schools can accommodate those parents' beliefs, and would be much more likely to be accommodating than public schools.

The next chapter uses hypothetical situations to discuss the specifics of how charter schools can accommodate, though not endorse, religion. These hypothetical question focus on how charter schools affect the balance between parental rights and states power with respect to directing children's education.

CHAPTER 4

HYPOTHETICAL RELIGION-BASED CHARTER SCHOOLS

WHY EXAMINE THE CONSTITUTIONALITY OF RELIGIOUS CHARTER SCHOOLS?

Chapter one posited several reasons for examining the constitutionality of religion-based charter schools. These reasons fall into two categories describing the future of religious charter schools: inevitability and uniqueness. Religious charter schools may be inevitable because the number of charter schools is increasing; some states are likely to eventually allow some types of religious charters; religious parents are often motivated toward novel educational possibilities; and religious organizations could try to circumnavigate barriers to opening charter schools. Additionally, recent Supreme Court cases invite the argument that excluding religious charters may be unconstitutional under the Free Speech Clause.

Religion-based charter schools also pose unique policy and legal questions because charter schools are a singular reform method. The prospect of religious charter schools exposes the conflicting interests of parents and the state vis-à-vis education. Charter schools also cause us to reexamine the state's obligation toward education. Additionally, the factual basis for allowing aid (vouchers) to religious private schools differs from the phenomenon of religious charter schools. Therefore, any reasoning about vouchers does not directly apply to charters; although such reasoning is,

Religious Charter Schools: Legalities and Practicalites, pp. 91–135
Copyright © 2007 by Information Age Publishing
All rights of reproduction in any form reserved.

of course, relevant. The recent Supreme Court voucher case (*Zelman v. Simmons-Harris*, 2002), consequently, did not answer the questions that arise when one contemplates religion-based charter schools.

Private schools are overwhelmingly religious: charter schools are overwhelmingly secular and will probably be for some time. Private schools are certainly private actors: charter schools are nearly certainly state actors. Lastly, the Supreme Court's Establishment Clause jurisprudence, as discussed in chapter 3, clearly distinguishes between vouchers (a private choice program) and charters (a per-capita aid program) (*Mitchell v. Helms*, 2000).

It is of course possible, albeit unlikely, that courts may ultimately find charter schools in some states to be private actors. A private school that receives 90% of its funding from public sources in nevertheless not a state actor for purposes of federal laws that prohibit state actors from violating constitutional rights (*Rendell-Baker v. Kohn*, 1982). However, charter schools are created by the states as public schools and are therefore almost certainly state actors, which the majority of this chapter takes for granted. The possibility of charter schools as private actors will be discussed later in this chapter.

For all of these reasons, this book examines the constitutionality of religion-based charter schools.

WHY HYPOTHETICAL SITUATIONS?

Hypothetical situations will be used in this chapter to discuss the constitutionality of religious charter schools. The three hypothetical situations, briefly, are schools of the following types: a morally-based school without mandatory prayer or religion classes, founded by coreligionists; a half-time secular school; and a denominational school operated by a religious organization with optional or mandatory prayer and religion classes.

Courts could examine the constitutionality of religion-based charter schools in one of two ways. First, if a state allowed religious charters to form, a court would address whether the statute violates the Establishment Clause. Second, a court could address whether a specific charter school or a specific action by a charter school violates the constitution.

Because states currently ban religious charters from forming, the second type of case is far more likely in the near future. These are the types of charter schools that Vickie Frost and other religious parents are likely to open. Consequently, a court would address the constitutionally of an actual religion-based charter school. The hypothetical situations provide a starting point for the legal questions addressed; however, some of the analysis alters the facts of the hypothetical situations.

Although the Supreme Court has created a distinct demarcation line between religious high schools and colleges, courts have analyzed elementary and high schools using the same legal standard. Thus, the hypothetical situations do not specify whether the school is an elementary school, a middle school, or a high school. Although it may one day be argued that a different standard should apply to each, this book accepts the present analysis.

Currently, states do not allow specifically religious charter schools to form. Because of the nature of the hypothetical situations, some of them would probably be permitted under some existing charter statutes; other hypothetical situations, however, would not. For the purpose of the analysis of this paper, I assume that each hypothetical school discussed is permitted under a general state charter statute that allows any charter school to form, whether or not it is religious. A state constitution can be more protective against the establishment of religion and many of them are. States cannot protect against the establishment of religion to the extent that it infringes on other federal constitutional rights. This book cannot address every state constitution and is not meant to provide legal advice.

The hypotheticals illustrate that the state may choose to shift some of its power over education to parents. With regard to religion, however, the state can only shift the power to create schools that accommodate parents' beliefs, but not schools that endorse parents' beliefs. The powers conferred on families will enable parents like those disaffected who sued in *Mozert v. Hawkins* (1987) to create religion-based charter schools that meet their most important needs.

MORALLY-BASED SCHOOL FOUNDED BY CORELIGIONISTS

Based on theistic morality, this charter school teaches no particular religious doctrines and has no mandatory prayer. It certainly does not discriminate on the basis of religion and no profession of any kind of faith is required. Even atheists are welcome. Every parent, however, must understand that the morality envisioned by this school is not based on nontheistic values or general notions of right. The values taught are those espoused by various religions as serving the good because that is why the Creator put man on earth.

The school forms after a group of people at a church, synagogue, mosque, temple or other house of worship become friends. (For the sake of brevity, I will use the word "church" through the rest of this paper to refer to any house of worship.) After services, one chapter complains about an incident at the local public school. Soon parents are spouting a list of complaints about the school. It does not teach proper values.

Children do not show their teachers proper respect. There is not enough homework. The work is too easy. The children are tracked, but the different classes cover the same level of material.

Some parents have children who also attend after-school religious programs. Some of their children attend soccer or other little league sports. A few parents mention that they considered sending their children to private school, but that it is too expensive because they have four or five children.

Eventually one of the parents recommends that they form a nonprofit corporation and explore the possibility of opening a charter school. The primary mission of the school would be to teach proper values like respect, honesty, integrity, chastity, fidelity, and prudence, along with a tracked, academically rigorous curriculum. Although the school would not be based on any particular religious tenets and would not discriminate on the basis of religion, the initial board would be comprised of members of the same church. The founders intend to advertise heavily at churches of their denomination.

The moral propositions taught would be based on universal notions of good. Some parents want the school to offer optional prayer, others want no prayer, while a third group wants mandatory prayer. After a discussion, the founding parents decide to have a room available for voluntary prayer before first period.

The seven questions addressed by the morally-based school generally address the issues of formation, mission, and control over the staff. The following legal issues are presented by this hypothetical. (1) Can coreligionists form a charter school? (2) Can morality-based general propositions of good be taught in a charter school? (3) Can a charter school teach values espoused by coreligionists? (4) Can a charter school teach a course in the relationship between religion and morality? (5) Can a charter school have religious criteria for staff? (6) Can a charter school limit a teacher's right to express different worldviews? (7) Can a charter school offer optional prayer?

Can Coreligionists Form a Charter School?

In 1994, in *Board of Education v. Grumet*, the Supreme Court held unconstitutional a New York State statute that made the Village of Kiryas Joel, an exclusively Satmar Hassidic community, into a school district. The New York State legislature created the school district so that the community would not have to pay the extraordinary costs to educate their children designated handicapped and entitled to services under the Individuals with Disabilities Education Act.

The community overwhelmingly sends its children to religious schools. The children were unable to receive special-needs services at public schools because of the "panic, fear and trauma [they] suffered in leaving their own community and being with people whose ways were so different" (*Board of Education v. Wieder*, 1988, 527 N.E.2d 767, 770).

The Supreme Court held that although the statute had a secular purpose, providing eligible children with a special-needs education, it was an unconstitutional delegation of civic authority to a religious group (*Board of Education v. Grumet*, 1994). First, the state delegated the power to operate a school board to a religious monopoly by special act. Second, there were no means of insuring that other groups similarly situated would be given the same benefit by the state.

It is unconstitutional to delegate civic powers to a religious authority. For example, the Supreme Court held unconstitutional granting churches the power to veto liquor licenses within 100 feet of their buildings (*Larkin v. Grendel's Den, Inc.*, 1982). The granting of power to the people of the Village was not distinguishable to the plurality. The difference between a constitutional and unconstitutional delegation of power lies in the definition of the recipients of the delegation. A government's purposeful delegation on the basis of religion is unconstitutional, while a delegation on principles neutral to religion, to individuals whose religious identities are incidental to their receipt of civic authority is constitutional. Because this delegation was on the basis of religion, it was unconstitutional. The plurality, however, noted that the fatal fact was not that the town was composed entirely of adherents of a particular sect, but that the State purposefully, by special act, had delegated power to the adherents of a religious sect.

Consequently, it would not be unconstitutional for coreligionists to form a charter school under a neutral charter statute. The Court would allow the Satmars of Kiryas Joel to form a school district based on a neutral state statute (*Board of Education v. Grumet*, 1994, 512 U.S. 687, 729-730). Therefore, the Constitution allows a secular charter school to form with a board composed of members of a single religious faith. Moreover, Justice Scalia in his dissent pointed out that several school districts across the country are made up of 100% coreligionists. If coreligionists can form a school district, they can form a charter school, since a charter school is similar in scope to a school district.

Board of Education v. Grumet (1994) was decided by a plurality of the Court. A plurality exists when the Justices agree on an outcome, but not the reasoning. Although six justices agreed that the school district was unconstitutional, only four justices agreed with the plurality opinion, which was written by Justice Souter.

Justice Kennedy, who was one of the Justices who agreed with the out-come but disagreed with the reasoning of the plurality, wrote that the only constitutional problem was that the district was created by a special enact-ment instead of a neutral law. In *Rosenberger v. University of Virginia* (1995), Justice Kennedy incorporated his reasoning from the *Grumet* decision into his opinion for the Court.

> We have held that the guarantee of neutrality is respected, not offended, when the government, following neutral criteria and evenhanded policies, extends benefits to recipients whose ideologies and viewpoints, including religious ones, are broad and diverse. (515 U.S. 819, 838)

The dissenting justices in *Rosenberger* disagreed, finding that "Evenhand-edness is therefore a prerequisite to further enquiry into the constitution-ality of a doubtful law, but evenhandedness goes no further. It does not guarantee success under the Establishment Clause" (515 U.S. 819, 879).

The difference between Justice Kennedy, who wrote the majority in *Rosenberger*, and Justice Souter, who wrote the plurality in *Grumet*, is that for Justice Kennedy a statute's neutrality enables coreligionists to derive a benefit from it. For Justice Souter, that is only half of the analysis.

According to the plurality in *Grumet* (1994), the Satmar school district was unconstitutional because it was created by a special act and conse-quently there was no guaranty that the state would create school districts for other religious minorities similarly situated. Because charter statutes set forth neutral criteria for charter school formation generally, this con-stitutional problem would not exist if a religious group formed a charter school as in the hypothetical. Because the state is not creating a single charter school to service a particular religious community's needs, there is no issue of whether the state would create another charter school for another religious group.

Since the state did not act for the religious group in creating charter schools, there is no issue of it needing to repeat its action for other reli-gious minorities. A group of coreligionists can form a charter school so long as the group's charter fits the specific criteria set by the state. This analysis assumes that a state's chartering agent would apply the criteria without favoring or disfavoring particular religious groups. Such discrimi-nation is also prohibited by the Constitution.

A final issue remains. Could a state create a charter system that spe-cifically encouraged coreligionists to form charter schools? It is highly unlikely that such a statute would be constitutional, since its purpose is to assist coreligionists and does not include other philosophical minori-ties (*Texas Monthly, Inc. v. Bullock*, 1989). Consequently, such an act would breach both the purpose and effect prongs of the *Lemon* (1971) test.

By contrast, a statute that, for example, allowed all religious minorities to form charter schools for the purpose of providing special education, would have a secular legislative purpose, since its purpose is to provide special-needs children from religious minorities with an education. Even though at first glance such a statute would seem to have the primary effect of advancing religion, it is not clear whether it would be unconstitutional. Such a programs' constitutionality depends on the distinction between *Walz v. Tax Commission* (1970) and *Texas Monthly v. Bullock* (1989).

Walz (1970) held constitutional a tax exemption for property held by religious organizations for the sole purpose of worship. *Texas Monthly* (1989) held unconstitutional a sales tax exemption for religious periodicals. Tax exemptions have been analyzed using the same analysis as other benefits. The difference between the two cases was that the property tax exemption was one of many tax exemptions for property, which included libraries, hospitals, and playgrounds. The sales tax exemption, however, was solely for religious periodicals.

A state could pass three types of laws allowing people to form charter schools for the purpose of providing special education. The law could apply to religious groups, religious or philosophical groups, or make no reference to religion. A charter statute that allowed charters to form to provide special-needs children from religious minorities with an education would be unconstitutional if it was the only way to open a charter school that served special-needs children.

Additionally, a statute allowing religious minorities to form charter schools to provide special education would be unconstitutional unless the statute also allowed philosophical minorities to form charter schools for the same purposes. Thus, a charter statute that permits coreligionists to form charter schools is constitutional if coreligionists are one of many groups allowed to form charter schools under the statute. A statute that only applied to coreligionists is not neutral because it defines applicants on the basis of religion and has an unconstitutional effect. Such a statute, however, is highly unlikely to be passed by a state legislature.

Can Morality-based General Propositions Constitutionally be Taught in a Charter School?

In this hypothetical, parents want values taught for secular reasons (e.g., students do not show their teachers proper respect). Parents also form the school because they are concerned with the low academic level of the local public school. This combination of reasons illustrates that parents are not forming the school for the sole purpose of teaching specific religious values, but rather because they are dissatisfied with their public school for a number of reasons.

It is possible, however, that parents who are generally satisfied with their public school in terms of its academics and the behavior of their children may choose to form a charter school for the sole purpose of teaching morality. Would such a school be constitutional?

One author, who writes about character education, asks the provocative question "Can We Be Good Without God?" (Tinder, 1989). From the Constitutional standpoint, there is a different question: Is the purpose to teach about good or to teach about God? It is clear that nonsectarian, nonreligious character education is constitutional in the same way that nonsectarian, nonreligious benedictions and invocations are constitutional. However, moral education already exists a place in our classrooms (Nylen, 1990). The moral is woven into the very fabric of classroom life, e.g., cheating is banned and punished (Wynne & Ryan, 1997, p. 108).

While the wisdom of teaching about values may certainly be questioned, teaching about values is not unconstitutional, just as teaching about religion is not unconstitutional (*Edwards v. Aguillard*, 1987). Teaching values, without the purpose of teaching religion, is certainly constitutional.

In one case, the 11th Circuit Court of Appeals overturned a district court's order to ban the use of 44 textbooks approved by the state of Alabama for the use in public schools (*Smith v. Board of Commissioners*, 1987). The district judge had held that the textbooks unconstitutionally advanced the religion of Secular Humanism and unconstitutionally excluded the advancements of Christianity. The appellate court held that the district court was in error in its conclusion that the textbooks advanced Secular Humanism and inhibited Christianity.

The appellate court also viewed the Establishment Clause requirement of neutrality in narrower terms than the district court. The "religious" content of the textbooks had to be viewed "in light of the overall context in which it occurs." As the Supreme Court had said years earlier,

> The "Establishment" Clause does not ban federal or state regulation of conduct whose reason or effect merely happens to coincide or harmonize with the tenets of some or all religions. In many instances, the Congress or state legislatures conclude that the general welfare of society, wholly apart from any religious considerations, demands such regulation. Thus, for temporal purposes, murder is illegal. (*McGowan v. Maryland*, 1961, 366 U.S. 420, 442)

Thus, teaching values, even values that coincide with religious beliefs, does not violate the Establishment Clause. If, however, those values, in

light of the context of the education, begin to constitute an overt endorsement of a religion or religion generally, then teaching those values is
unconstitutional. The teacher must be careful to teach the value, and not
the religion, because teaching the religion is an endorsement of the religion (*Hall v. Board of Education*, 1981).

Can a Charter School Teach Values Espoused by Coreligionists?

Having addressed the issues of coreligionists forming a charter and
teaching values in a charter school, the next logical question is whether
the combination of values having a basis in religion and the charter
school being founded by coreligionists would make the school unconstitutional. The Eighth Circuit Court of Appeals held that a school district
could open a school primarily for coreligionists that departed from the
regular district curriculum in that it used no televisions, radios, or computers (*Stark v. Indep. School Dist.*, 1997). The school primarily catered to
the children of a religious sect, the Brethren, who shunned technology,
but also served some non-Brethren children.

The school had several secular purposes besides facilitating the secular
education of the Brethren children. The district financially benefited
from the operation of the school. The school saved the district the costs of
bussing the children who chose to attend the school. Additionally, the
school and district gained state aid based on the fact that the Brethren
parents might otherwise have home-schooled their children (*Stark*, 123
F.3d 1068, 1070).

The school rented the school's classroom from a member of the Brethren and limited the use of computers and other electronic equipment in
the school to the extent allowable by law. The parents were allowed to
remove their children from lessons that violated their religious beliefs, but
parents had no more input over the school curriculum than in other
schools.

Although the Brethren did not operate the school at issue, the case is
useful because many of the values within the curriculum were adjusted to
fit the needs of a religious group. The purpose of the school was not to
teach particular values, but rather to teach within a value system to
accommodate those children's religious needs. Moreover, the purpose was
to provide the children with a public secular education. Thus, the issue
was one of religious effect. The court held that the school did not violate
the Establishment Clause because although the school was created in part
to accommodate the needs of a religious group, it did not turn away children who were not Brethren. Moreover, because the school provided some

technology to non-Brethren students, the school did not alter its curriculum to conform to the sectarian needs of a religious group.

Merely respecting specific religious values within a curriculum, as in the hypothetical, is not adapting the curriculum to meet the needs of a religious group. Little is being removed from the curriculum. Values naturally exist as a part of the educational process and this school merely places a greater emphasis upon values important to the charter founders.

There is, of course, a danger that a board of coreligionists would choose values specific to their religion. However, if the combination of teaching values and a board of coreligionists made a school unconstitutional, that would create a perverse result, meaning that a school operated by coreligionists could not teach the same values as a charter school with board members with a mix of religions. In his dissent to *Board of Education v. Grumet* (1994), Justice Scalia noted that many counties contained 90% or greater coreligionists (512 U.S. 687, 736).

If the charter's values curriculum were a pretext for endorsing or indoctrinating religion, then the school would be unconstitutional. Otherwise, coreligionists can operate a charter school with the purpose of teaching values.

Coreligionists cannot form a charter school with the purpose of teaching religion. There may be a fine line between general values found within religion and specific religious values, but the constitution permits a school based on one, but not the other. Even if in theory coreligionists can separate their religious values and their religion, in practice this may prove impossible. One district tried to teach a course about religion, which is permissible; however, in practice it was an unconstitutional course conveying a religious message (*Wiley v. Franklin*, 1980). Coreligionists trying to form a school based on values may have the same problem, but forming such a school is not per se unconstitutional.

A charter school operating under a system of values is significantly different from an entire district operating from a value viewpoint. A charter school is a single school within a choice system. Thus, the parents who attend the school choose to teach their children those values. Such a situation is substantially different from a school district choosing a set of values to teach all the district children. The case involving the Brethren is so illuminating because the district was operating a second school to accommodate the needs of a segment of its population. The district was not forcing all of the children to attend a school that limited technology for the sake of a religious group.

Lastly, the state must provide coreligionists with some level of accommodation based on their religious beliefs (*Wisconsin v. Yoder*, 1972). The degree of accommodation and whether that accommodation is required by the Constitution is rooted in the history and needs of the religion (*Wisconsin v. Yoder*). The Supreme Court held that the old order Amish could not be required to formally school their children beyond age 14. A charter school could not have settled the issue since the Amish did not want their children to attend any school, even private school. Although the *Yoder* (1972) case was a narrow decision, it stands for the principle that in extreme circumstances the state must accommodate the values of a religion even when the state is pursuing a neutral, secular policy. The decision does not mean that the state must allow a values-based charter school to form, but the reasoning does support the proposition that the state should consider parents' values and religious beliefs when making broad educational policy decisions that affect religious minorities.

Can a Charter School Teach a Course in the Relationship Between Religion and Morality?

Most of the cases involving teaching religion in public schools have confronted teaching the Christian Bible. A Bible literature course is unconstitutional if it has the primary effect of advancing religion. Therefore, a Bible course taught from the Christian perspective has been held by courts to be unconstitutional.

In one such case, a federal District Court Judge granted an injunction to stop a voluntary Bible class at an elementary school because the instruction in the class was sectarian and had the primary effect of advancing religion (*Hall v. Board of School Commissioners of Conecuh County,* 1981). The course included several songs that "unapologetically stated Christian dogma" (*Doe v. Human,* 1989, 725 F. Supp. 1503, 1506).

That does not mean that all courses about the Bible or about religion are unconstitutional. One of the clearest pronouncements by the Supreme Court in favor of teaching about religion in public schools occurred in *Abington v. Schempp* (1963), a case that held unconstitutional a Pennsylvania statute that required schools to read from the Bible each day:

> It might well be said that one's education is not complete without a study of comparative religion or the history of religion and its relationship to the advancement of civilization. (374 U.S. 203, 225)

Thus, the Supreme Court has acknowledged a distinction between teaching religion and teaching *about* religion. Teaching about religion is constitutional so long as the course does not endorse the religion taught. A course that surveyed religions for the purpose of finding universal values would be constitutional so long as it did not endorse religion generally.

The values would be the primary focus of the course and it would be teaching about the religions and about the values.

Can a Charter School Have Religious Criteria for Staff?

No state organization, including charter schools, may have a religious criterion for participation (*Torcaso v. Watkins*, 1991). The Supreme Court has held that it was unconstitutional for a state to require that a notary public profess a belief in god. Accordingly, a charter school could not require teachers to profess any particular belief (*Torcaso v. Watkins*, 1991). Charter schools are able to have religiously neutral behavior criteria for staff that do not impinge on the staff's freedom of speech (*East Hartford Education Association v. Board of Education*, 1977).

If charter schools were held to be private rather than public entities (i.e., nonstate actors), and the constitution allowed denominational charters to form, it is still not clear whether charter schools could have religious criteria for staff. Title VII prohibits employers from discriminating against employees on the basis of religion. Title VII's definition of "religion" includes all aspects of religious observance and practice, as well as belief. Religious criteria for staff would certainly fall under this prohibition.

Title VII, however, exempts some religious organizations from this prohibition:

> This subchapter shall not apply to ... a religious corporation, association, educational institution, or society with respect to the employment of individuals of a particular religion to perform work connected with the carrying on by such corporation, association, educational institution, or society of its activities. (42 U.S.C. § 2000e-1(a))

This exemption is constitutional (*Corp. of Presiding Bishop of the Church of Jesus Christ of Latter-Day Saints v. Amos*, 1987). Additionally, schools may discriminate on the basis of hiring when supported by a religious organization or the curriculum is religious (42 U.S.C. § 2000e-2(e)(2)).

These exemptions do not give religious schools carte blanche to discriminate against employees (*Boyd v. Harding Academy of Memphis, Inc.*, 1996). For example, a religious school may discriminate against employees for having premarital sex when it is contrary to its religious precepts, but it cannot use premarital sex as a pretext for discriminating against a teacher who is pregnant. A school may discriminate for religious reasons (i.e., the belief that it is wrong to have premarital sex), but a school cannot discriminate on the basis of a secular reason (i.e., being pregnant) (*Boyd v. Harding Academy of Memphis, Inc.*; *Cline v. Catholic Diocese of Toledo*, 2000).

To qualify for a religious exemption, a school must be genuinely religious, not merely affiliated with a religious organization (*Equal Employment Opportunity Commission v. Kamehameha Schools/Bishop Estate*, 1993). In *Kamehameha*, the court held that a school could not require that all on-campus teachers be Protestant when the curriculum of the school did not propagate religion.

Assuming charter schools are public schools, charters cannot have religious criteria for staff under any circumstances. However, if the constitution permits denominational charters to form and charter schools are not state actors (see discussion later in this chapter), then the federal Constitution may not apply; charter schools, therefore, may be exempt from the nondiscrimination requirements of Title VII. For the exemption to apply to hiring practices of a charter school, the school would have to be explicitly religious and satisfy one of two criteria: Either the chartering organization must be a religious organization itself (a religious organization operating a secular school would probably not qualify for an exemption under the act), or the curriculum of the charter school must propagate religion (42 U.S.C. § 2000e-2). Neither is possible under present law. States, moreover, are unlikely to allow such charter schools to form.

Can a Charter School Limit a Teacher's Right to Express Different Worldviews?

A public school may restrict a teacher's in-school speech so long as the administration's actions are reasonably related to legitimate pedagogical concerns (*Miles v. Denver Public Schools*, 1991). The Supreme Court has acknowledged that teachers, regardless of tenure, have a right to free speech (*Mt. Healthy City Sch. Dist. Bd. of Ed. v. Doyle*, 1977; *Pickering v. Board of Education of Township High School District 205*, 1968). The Supreme Court, however, has not established a clear standard for when a school may penalize a teacher for her speech. The test used by lower courts in teacher-speech cases comes from the test the Court has applied to school-sponsored, student speech (*Hazelwood Sch. Dist. v. Kuhlmeier*, 1988). Lower courts have reasoned that when a teacher is in the classroom, it is a school-sponsored activity not in a public forum (*Miles v. Denver Public Schools*, 1991).

Teachers have been successfully disciplined for stating in class that the quality of the school had declined (*Miles v. Denver Public Schools*), discussing abortion during a biology class (*Ward v. Hickey*, 1993), and allowing students to use profanity in assignments (*Lacks v. Ferguson Reorganized School Dist.*, 1998). Unconstitutional action was taken when a school transferred a teacher who selected a controversial play (*Boring v. Buncombe County Board of Education*, 1996). Courts have also upheld administrations that forbade teachers from discussing religion in their classroom or during their office hours (*Peloza v. Capistrano*, 1994) and that ordered a teacher to remove religious books and posters from a classroom library (*Roberts v. Madigan*, 1990).

Public schools cannot, absent extreme circumstance, discipline a teacher for comments made outside of school (*Pickering v. Board of Education of Township High School District 205*, 1968). Schools, for example, may not discipline teachers for advocating homosexual activity or admitting homosexuality outside the classroom (*National Gay Task Force v. Board of Education of the City of Oklahoma City*, 1984; *Weaver v. Nebo School District*, 1998). Teachers can be dismissed for participation in organizations that advocate legalizing intergenerational sexual activity (*Melzer v. Board of Education*, 2003). Teachers can, of course, be disciplined for general misconduct (*Hearne v. Illinois State Board of Educ.*, 1999).

Schools have greater leeway when hiring a teacher than when disciplining a teacher who is already working at a school. The right to free speech is not dependent on a teacher's property right in employment (*Perry v. Sindermann*, 1972). Contractual employment, however, gives a teacher an additional due process right that must be protected (*Board of Regents v. Roth*, 1972). Schools do not have unlimited power when hiring teachers, which is illustrated by the numerous cases striking down loyalty oaths, including such oaths for teachers (*Baggett v. Bullitt*, 1964; *Cramp v. Board of Public Instruction of Orange County Fllorida*, 1961; *Wieman v. Updegraff*, 1952).

A review of cases reveals an easily articulated principle. Schools may demand that teachers' speech in the classroom conform to any reasonable rules; however, schools cannot legitimately prevent teachers from expressing their views outside of school, unless it seriously affects the teacher's ability to function as a role model. A charter school may, therefore, demand that a teacher conform to its mission and worldview while in the classroom, but cannot, absent extreme circumstance, discipline a teacher for comments made outside of school.

Can a Charter School Offer Optional Prayer?

Lee v. Weisman (1992) squarely addressed the issue of school-sponsored prayer in public schools. (The Court has treated nondenominational and denomination prayer more or less equally.) In *Lee*, the Supreme Court held unconstitutional a middle school principal's inviting a rabbi to deliver a nondenominational prayer at graduation. Such a prayer was held coercive regardless of the fact that graduation attendance was voluntary:

Finding no violation under these circumstances would place objectors in the dilemma of participating, with all that implies, or protesting. We do not address whether that choice is acceptable if the affected citizens are mature adults, but we think the State may not, consistent with the Establishment Clause, place primary or secondary children in this position. (505 U.S. 577, 593)

In *Santa Fe v. Doe* (2000), the Supreme Court expanded the principles in *Lee* to include district (or school) policies that encourage student-led prayer, holding unconstitutional a policy that had students voting whether prayer would occur at sports events and graduation. The problem with the policy in *Santa Fe v. Doe* was that the school, by asking the students to vote on prayer, rather than other secular invocations, implicitly endorsed prayer regardless of how the students voted.

A public school cannot authorize prayer in any situation. Prayer must be wholly voluntary to students. This would include any prayer, Bible reading, or moment of silence announced over the school intercom. Moments of silence for secular reasons such as memorials are constitutional. Additionally, students who are chosen for secular reasons (e.g., valedictorian, senior class president) to make a speech at graduation can include prayer in their speeches (*Adler v. Duval County*, 2000).

Prayer offered at a charter school would be different in two ways from the prayers at issue in *Lee* (1992) or *Santa Fe* (2000). First, the children attending the school would be at the school by their or their parents' choice, knowing that the school would have prayer. The Supreme Court has not treated the choices of students and parents differently when examining the Establishment Clause. In fact the Supreme Court, as a general rule, has noted that parents have an interest in bringing up their children in their faith and culture.

Furthermore, the prayer offered at the school could more easily be made voluntary. Prayer at graduation or sports games is necessarily coercive because the students at graduation and the game are subjected to the prayer. Prayer that is offered in a separate room on the school site does not have a captive audience. Schools would also have to make available rooms for meditation or philosophical reflection (*Texas Monthly, Inc. v. Bullock*, 1989). Although students might feel peer pressure to attend prayer in designated rooms, that pressure would not be attributable to the state because the rooms are available to all.

The other cases involving prayer, Bible readings, and moments of silence addressed by the Supreme Court all involved state statutes requiring or encouraging the activities in all schools across the state (*Abington v. Schempp*, 1963; *Chamberlin v. Dade County*, 1964; *Engel v. Vitale*, 1962; *Wallace v. Jaffree*, 1985). Moreover, prayer at a school can vary in a number of ways. A member of the clergy, teachers, administrators, or students themselves could lead it. If a teacher or an administrator led voluntary prayer, or invited a member of the clergy to lead, the prayer would almost certainly be unconstitutional because the prayer could be attributed to the school and, therefore, the state (*Roberts v. Madigan*, 1990; *Zorach v. Clauson*, 1952).

The prayer is unconstitutional even if the attendance is wholly voluntary because on school grounds teachers are considered representatives of the school administration (*Peloza v. Capistrano*, 1994). However, if students developed a prayer group and they invited the clergy to attend and lead, it would be constitutional so long as there was a general policy that allowed people from outside school to attend student groups. A policy of inviting outsiders that was limited to clergy would be unconstitutional.

Under the federal Equal Access Act, public schools must allow students to form after-school clubs once the school allows noncurricular clubs. This includes religious clubs (*Board of Education v. Mergens*, 1990). Thus, religious activity by students, on school grounds, is not attributed to the school and is, therefore, constitutional. Students of course have the right to exercise their religious beliefs. The issue is whether the school would *endorse* students' prayer by providing a room in which to pray.

A charter school could furnish a room in a number of ways. A school could provide one room for prayer, allow students to use a room if they had a fixed number in a prayer group, or generally provide rooms to all students who want to pray. So long as the policy was neutral between religions, and between religion and nonreligion, it would be constitutional. The school would not have to provide a room to students who were atheists and wanted a club during those hours, but would have to provide a room to atheist students who wanted to meditate or gather to discuss philosophical views (*Texas Monthly, Inc. v. Bullock*, 1989). Of course if students wanted to form a religion club, then the school would have to allow atheists to form clubs also.

Prayer at a charter school can take many forms. Because charter schools are open to all students they cannot permit coercive prayer that all students are subjected to, such as over the loudspeaker. Charters can provide students with a place to pray, so long as the prayer is always student-led and the rules regarding use of the facilities are neutral toward religion.

HALF-TIME SECULAR SCHOOL

Several parents approach a clergyman and ask him if the church can start a school. He tells each of them the same thing. The church barely has the funds and facilities to support its after-school program. More-over, the after-school program is not successful because by the time the students arrive they are tired and are not interested in learning religion.

Establishing a private school interests parents because they are disaffected with the local public school, where they have had little success making the school adapt to their needs. The parents' perception is based on the large class size at the public school (30) and their sense that the teachers do not know the full capability of individual students. Additionally, many parents are afraid that their children will be swept up into the drug culture that is prevalent among some of the students at the public school. Many parents want to send their children to a private school, but cannot afford the high tuition.

One of the parents recommends that the clergyman look into starting a charter school. The clergyman realizes that a charter school could suit the requirements of the parents and at the same time help him coordinate a successful religious-school program. He contacts other ministers around the city to create a planning committee for a charter school. The question arises whether it would be financially beneficial to operate the school on the premises of an existing religious school.

The proposed school would meet from eight in the morning until one in the afternoon, the minimum amount of time that the school could be open and allow for a moderately flexible schedule while still fulfilling state academic graduation requirements. The administration strongly assumes, but does not require, that students will attend after-school religious classes. Students are required to attend an after-school program, which can be academic, athletic, theatrical, or religious. Students are not permitted to go home and watch television or hold a job immediately after school, although they are free to do so after an after-school program. The school's mission is to allow students the opportunity to explore religious and secular extracurricular activities without extending the day excessively. Most children (90%) opt to attend after-school religious programs at one of three neighborhood churches.

The following legal issues are presented by this hypothetical. The focus of the four questions in this hypothetical is on the purpose and practicalities of forming such a school. (1) Can a charter school form for the primary purpose of allowing students' ease of access to religious education? (2) Can a charter school form to provide students, who would otherwise attend faith-based, with a free, secular public education? (3) Can clergy sit on the board of a charter school? (4) Can a charter school share facilities with a religious school?

Relevant Supreme Court Decisions

The background for the legal issues presented by this hypothetical is found in two Supreme Court decisions that directly address the issue of students leaving school for religious instruction: *McCollum v. Board of Education*, decided in 1948, and *Zorach v. Clauson*, decided in 1952. Both *McCollum* and *Zorach* were decided before the Supreme Court developed the *Lemon* framework and neither case addressed coordinated instruction in a charter school. Nevertheless, because these cases address the issue of coordinating religious and secular instruction directly, they serve as a natural starting-point to examine this hypothetical.

McCollum v. Board of Education (1948) was the first Establishment Clause case that the Supreme Court heard after *Everson v. Board of Education* (1947). Illinois had a compulsory education law that required that students attend either public schools or private (including religious) schools that met educational standards fixed by the state. Religious organizations of various faiths created the Champaign Council on Religious Education, to provide religious education in the Champaign County School District.

> Jewish, Roman Catholic, and a few of the Protestant faiths ... obtained permission from the Board of Education to offer classes in religious instruction to public school pupils in grades four to nine inclusive. Classes were made up of pupils whose parents signed printed cards requesting that their children be permitted to attend; they were held weekly, thirty minutes for the lower grades, forty-five minutes for the higher. The council employed the religious teachers at no expense to the school authorities, but the instructors were subject to the approval and supervision of the superintendent of schools. The classes were taught in three separate religious groups by Protestant teachers, Catholic priests, and a Jewish rabbi, although for the past several years there have apparently been no classes instructed in the Jewish religion. Classes were conducted in the regular classrooms of the school building. Students who did not choose to take the religious instruction were not released from public school duties; they were required to leave their classrooms and go to some other place in the school building for pursuit of their secular studies. On the other hand, students who were released from secular study for the religious instructions were required to be present at the religious classes. Reports of their presence or absence were to be made to their secular teachers. (*McCollum v. Board of Education*, 333 U.S. 203, 208-09)

The Court did not address allegations that in "actual practice certain Protestant groups ... obtained an overshadowing advantage in the propagation of their faiths over other Protestant sects" and that "subtle pressures were brought to bear on the students to force them to participate" in the program. The Court held the program was an unconstitutional use of tax-supported property for religious instruction complicated by the close cooperation between the school authorities and the religious council in promoting religious education. Moreover, the Court squarely rejected the argument that the Establishment Clause only bars the state preferring one religion over another, but held that the state also cannot prefer religion over nonreligion or vice versa.

The main problem with the religious instruction at issue was that it occurred on public school grounds. The short amount of time spent in religious instruction was irrelevant as the constitutional difficulty was the imprimatur of the state. The way the Champaign Council on Religious Education and the Champaign School District Board designed the program endorsed, the religious instruction rather than merely accommodating the schedule so it could occur.

> If it were merely a question of enabling a child to obtain religious instruction with a receptive mind the 30 or 45 minutes could readily be found on Saturday or Sunday. If that were all, Champaign might have drawn upon the French system, known in its American manifestation as "dismissed time," whereby one school day is shortened to allow all children to go where they please, leaving those who so desire to go to a religious school. The momentum of the whole school atmosphere and school planning is presumably put behind religious instruction, as given in Champaign, precisely in order to secure for the religious instruction such momentum and planning. To speak of "released time" as being only half or three quarters of an hour is to draw a thread from a fabric. (*McCollum v. Board of Education*, 1948, 333 U.S. 203, 230-231, Frankfurter, J., concurring)

The program at issue in *Zorach v. Clauson* (1952) involved another program of "release time," a New York City program that permitted its public schools to release students during the school day. Students would leave the school buildings and go to religious centers for religious instruction or devotional services (*Zorach v. Clauson*, 343 U.S. 306, 308). The program involved neither public expense nor religious instruction on public school grounds. Moreover, the school authorities and teachers were neutral regarding the program and did not coerce or persuade students to participate in religious instruction.

The program had six features: students had to obtain permission from their parents or guardian to attend the program; students had to register for the training and provide schools with a copy of the registration; religious schools had to file weekly attendance reports; only 1 hour per week could be allotted to the training and it had to be at the end of the class session; the hour had to be the same for all religious schools participating in the program.

Justice Douglas, writing for the Court, upheld the program. He compared the permission required to attend the "release time" instruction with a religious parent sending a note so a student could be excused from school for a religious holiday. The public schools did "accommodate their schedules to a program of outside religious instruction," but it was a permissible accommodation (*Zorach v. Clauson*, 1952, 343 U.S. 306, 315).

Although the programs were not on public school grounds and did not use public funds, three Justices dissented on the grounds that the program was not substantially different than the one in *McCollum*. Justice Black accused the state of using "compulsory education laws to help religious sects get attendants presumably too unenthusiastic to go unless moved to do so by the pressure of this state machinery [and] manipulating its compulsory education laws to help religious sects get pupils" (*Zorach v. Clauson*, 1952, 343 U.S. 306, 318, Black, J., dissenting).

Consequently, to the dissenting Justices, the constitutional issue was not whether the program occurred on public school grounds, but rather whether the school schedule was changed specifically and exclusively to accommodate religious instruction. The dissenting Justices viewed such a system as inherently coercive.

> Of course a State may provide that the classes in its schools shall be dismissed, for any reason, or no reason, on fixed days, or for special occasions. The essence of this case is that the school system did not "close its doors" and did not "suspend its operations." There is all the difference in the world between letting the children out of school and letting some of them out of school into religious classes. If every one is free to make what use he will of time wholly unconnected from schooling required by law--those who wish sectarian instruction devoting it to that purpose, those who have ethical instruction at home, to that, those who study music, to that--then of course there is no conflict with the Fourteenth Amendment. (*Zorach v. Clauson*, 1952, 343 U.S. 306, 320, Frankfurter, J., dissenting)

Justice Frankfurter observed that the Court noted that "coercion in the abstract" would create an unconstitutional program, but that the record was devoid of such proof because of the procedural posture of the case. Moreover, Justice Frankfurter argued that such coercion was "inherent in the system." The majority and dissent disagreed whether the program was inherently coercive, but both acknowledged that actual coercion would be unconstitutional.

Can a Charter School Form For the Purpose of Allowing Students Ease of Access to Religious Education?

The general principle that can be derived from *McCollum* (1948) and *Zorach* (1952) is that religious instruction that occurs on site at a public school is unconstitutional while religious instruction that is off-site is constitutional. The Court followed a similar principle in *Wolman v. Walter* (1977), which held constitutional providing therapeutic services to special-needs students at private schools only so long as those services were provided in mobile units off the grounds of faith-based schools.

Providing secular services at a religious school and providing religious services at a public school both present problems. At the religious school, the danger is that the "pervasively-sectarian" environment will affect the way that the public employee performs her job (*Wolman v. Walter*, 1977, 433 U.S. 229, 247). At the public school, the danger is one of creating coercive pressure on students to participate in religious education, or religion generally.

When religious instruction is moved off school grounds, the state is merely permissibly accommodating religion by manipulating its schedule. As the Court stated in *Zorach* (1952), the state may encourage religious instruction or cooperates with religious authorities by adjusting the schedule of public events to sectarian needs. Thus, manipulating a school's schedule to allow for religious instruction is at face value constitutional.

Although today's Court would not state that "encouraging religious instruction" is the proper role of the state, the Court would acknowledge that schools may accommodate the religious needs of their students. The question arises, however, whether creating an entire school schedule to accommodate religious training would be constitutionally different from accommodating it by allowing students out early 1 hour per week. Additionally, it is somewhat unclear whether *Zorach* (1952) would be decided the same way today (*Lee v. Weisman*, 1992; *Texas Monthly v. Bullock*, 1989).

Justice Frankfurter, in his dissent to *Zorach* (1952), indicated that a half-day school would be constitutionally preferable to manipulating the schedule to accommodate religious classes. "Of course a State may provide that the classes in its schools shall be dismissed, for any reason, or no reason, on fixed days, or for special occasions" (*Zorach v. Clauson*, 343 U.S. 306, 320, Frankfurter, J., dissenting). Since the hypothetical school day is arranged so that it ends every day at 1:00, there is no constitutional issue. By ending the school day at a uniform time, the possibility of coercion is lessened (if not eliminated) because there is no attendance requirement at a religious program. Regular monitoring regarding attendance at a religious program would possibly constitute an unconstitutional "excessive entanglement."

A charter school can require that students attend an after-school program; a charter's philosophy can espouse that children need time to attend extracurricular activities. Some children would attend religious instruction; others might attend sports or music lessons. This would be a neutral criterion, and certainly a constitutional one, for operating a charter school (*Rosenberger v. University of Virginia*, 1995).

If, however, the school only allowed students to enroll if they attended religious programs after school, it is less likely that the school would be constitutional. Such a program would discriminate between religion and nonreligion, which is generally unconstitutional (*Texas Monthly, Inc. v. Bullock*, 1989). In *Texas Monthly v. Bullock*, Justice Blackmun pointed out "the Establishment Clause value suggests that a State may not give a tax break to those who spread the gospel that it does not also give to others who actively might advocate disbelief in religion" (489 U.S. 1, 26, Blackmun, J., concurring). Because the tax break was only available to religious periodicals in the state, the Texas statute, which blatantly favored religion, was not neutral. A charter school, however, could form using a neutral statute benefiting all parents who want to form schools, religious and nonreligious alike.

It is far from certain that a school that only enrolled students who attended religious after school programs would be unconstitutional. The hypothetical charter school described would merely use a neutral benefit for religious purposes. Similarly, different parents could form another charter school that let out early, but required attendance at nonreligious activities. Using the Court's recent vision of neutrality, such a benefit would be constitutional because the state statute allowing the school would itself be neutral (*Rosenberger v. University of Virginia*, 1995). The state is truly neutral allowing benefits to flow to religious and nonreligious alike even when the religions benefit directly (Monsma, 1993). The Constitution does not require that the beneficiaries of the state use their benefits neutrally, merely that the state be neutral when doling them out.

It seems unlikely that a school would exclude students whose parents wanted them to attend a secular after-school activity. First, such a school would invite a lawsuit challenging its constitutionality, unlike a school that did not have such exclusion. The philosophy of such a school would likely maintain that religious and secular education should be separate. The school would rely on the state to finance a secular education, meanwhile private organizations would provide a religious education. Parents when drafting the charter would also want to bear in mind that having the prospective charter refused for having a religious purpose will be considered if they later reapply for a charter (*McCreary County v. ACLU*, 2005).

Consequently, there would be little reason to exclude children who wanted to attend secular after-school activities. However, since experience shows that those who start independent schools, and those who choose them, are more often than not motivated by religious considerations, it is, of course, possible that parents would form a charter school that required attendance at a religious program after school. This is much less likely to be constitutional than a school that allowed students to attend both religious and nonreligious activities.

Can a Charter School Form to Provide Students, Who Would Otherwise Attend Religious Schools, With a Free, Secular Public Education?

In *Board of Education v. Grumet* (1994), the Supreme Court held unconstitutional a New York State statute that made the Village of Kiryas Joel, an exclusively Satmar Hassidic community, into a school district. The State created the school district so that the community would not have to pay the extraordinary costs to educate their children designated handicapped and who were entitled to services under the Individuals with Disabilities Education Act. The Supreme Court held that although the statute had a secular purpose, providing eligible children with a special-needs education, it was unconstitutional because it was a special enactment for the benefit of a religious group.

Rosenberger v. University of Virginia (1995) shifted the analysis from the financial benefit of the recipients to the neutrality of the statute, noting "that the guarantee of neutrality is respected, not offended, when the government, following neutral criteria and evenhanded policies, extends benefits to recipients whose ideologies and viewpoints, including religious ones, are broad and diverse" (*Rosenberger*, 515 U.S. 819, 839). Neutrality is the key aspect of the examination, not funding, because the government usually acts by spending money.

Were money the main criterion, then all benefits received by religion, including access to facilities, would be unconstitutional. The Supreme Court has held, there is no difference between a school using its funds when it gives access to its facilities, and a school paying a third-party contractor to operate the facility on its behalf.

Because any statute authorizing charter schools is presumed by this analysis to be neutral toward religion, a religious group could use that statute to receive the same benefit that a nonreligious group could. Namely, a religious group could use the statute to provide their children with a secular education. In such a situation the government is not funding religious practices, it is merely deferring the cost of a secular education, which is a permissible purpose under the Establishment Clause (*Committee for Public Education and Religious Liberty v. Nyquist*, 1973). The state's interest in providing an education to its populace has nothing to do with sectarian issues. Consequently, the state may provide a benefit to religious education as part of a neutral program, so long as benefiting religion generally is not the primary effect of the statute (*Mueller v. Allen*, 1983).

Can Clergy sit on the Board of a Charter School?

In *McDaniel v. Paty* (1978) the Supreme Court addressed the issue of whether a state could bar members of the clergy from serving as legislators or members of state constitutional conventions. The State of Tennessee asserted that the Establishment Clause justified the prohibition in order to maintain appropriate separation between church and state. The Court wholly rejected this contention:

> The essence of the rationale underlying the Tennessee restriction on ministers is that if elected to public office they will necessarily exercise their powers and influence to promote the interests of one sect or thwart the interests of another, thus pitting one against the others, contrary to the anti-establishment principle with its command of neutrality. However widely that view may have been held in the 18th century by many, including enlightened statesmen of that day, the American experience provides no persuasive support for the fear that clergymen in public office will be less careful of anti-establishment interests or less faithful to their oaths of civil office than their unordained counterparts. (*McDaniel v. Paty*, 435 U.S. 618, 628–629)

As the Court rejected the state's rationale for the law, the restriction's infringement on the free exercise of religion invalidated the prohibition.

In *Torcaso v. Watkins* (1961) the Court had previously held that the state could not require notaries, as a test of office, to profess a belief in God. Just as the state cannot prohibit religious officials from serving in public office, the state cannot limit public offices to those who profess certain religious beliefs. The Constitution directly states "no religious test shall ever be required as a Qualification to any Office or public Trust under the United States" (Article VI). The Court, however, also invalidated the Tennessee provision on the basis of the Free Exercise Clause. The state cannot limit officeholders based on their religious beliefs or ordination.

Consequently, members of the clergy cannot be excluded from sitting on the boards of charters. Nor can charters form that require one member [or all members] of its board be clergyman. The charter must be silent as to religious qualifications in terms of board membership. Clergy can also certainly sit on the committees that apply for charters.

Can a Charter School Share Facilities With a Religious School?

Since a clergyman initiates the hypothetical charter school to provide secular education as a supplement to religious education, it becomes necessary to explore whether a charter school could share facilities with a religious school. The Supreme Court has abandoned the assumption placing public employees at a faith-based school inevitably results in state-sponsored indoctrination or constitutes a "symbolic union between government and religion" (*Agostini v. Felton*, 1997, 521 U.S. 203, 223). Placing a public and religious school in the same building creates a similar risk of "symbolic union." Ten years ago, the inquiry would end there and such a relationship would probably be unconstitutional; now the answer is far from clear.

Public school districts often rent space to private religious schools. These are business contracts that involve two wholly separate entities. The most common instance is the state's renting out an unused building. Such arrangements are constitutional so long as there is no symbolic union or favoritism for particular schools or religions. A half-time charter school that rents space to a religious school in the afternoon is qualitatively different because a single charter is doing business with a single religious school sharing its only building.

A charter school that operated for a half-day could certainly rent out its building in the afternoon (*Lamb's Chapel v. Center Moriches*, 1993). Moreover, the school could rent out its building to religious organizations, so long as religious associations were not preferred over secular ones. The charter school in the hypothetical would, however, have a relationship with a single religious school. A single charter school renting its facilities in the afternoon to a faith-based school presents a different situation from a nonprofit corporation that ran several half-day charters renting out one of its school building during the afternoon.

What might be constitutional aid to a religion based charter school, may be an unconstitutional religious action taken by the state. Any action taken by a charter school is attributable to the state. In her concurrence to *Lynch v. Donnelly* (1984), Justice O'Connor wrote, "Every government practice must be judged in its unique circumstances to determine whether it constitutes an endorsement or disapproval of religion" (465 U.S. 668, 694). Although a majority of the Court has not adopted Justice O'Connor's view, it is a useful means of examining such situations.

In *Grand Rapids v. Ball* (1985) the Court examined two programs that furnished aid to private schools on school grounds; both programs were found unconstitutional. The Shared Time program offered classes to private school students on school grounds during the regular school day.

These were secular classes, chosen by the state, and taught by state employees. The Community Education program consisted of secular, enrichment classes available to children and adults that were taught by full-time teachers, overwhelmingly the same teachers who taught at faith-based schools.

Justice O'Connor, whose views became law in *Agostini v. Felton* (1997), considered the shared time program constitutional and Community Education program unconstitutional because religious schoolteachers, on the premises of the same private school, taught the Community Education courses. This created too great a risk that religion would be injected into the state-funded lessons (*Grand Rapids v. Ball*, 1985). Consequently, if the charter school and the private school shared employees, it would clearly be unconstitutional Justice O'Connor.

There are of course some permissible circumstances when a public school and religious school may rent facilities from one another. Often this is the case with special-needs students and sharing a facility is the most efficient use of resources. It is highly unlikely, however, that two schools could share the same building and many of the same students without creating the sort of symbolic union or entanglement that the Establishment Clause forbids.

Even if the constitution permitted a religiously-indoctrinating charter school, placing a secular charter school and a religious school in the same building is problematic because such an arrangement mixes secular and religious institutions. This result might appear illogical, but it fits within the framework of the "blurred, indistinct, and variable barrier" that is the Establishment Clause (*Lemon v. Kurtzman*, 1971, 403 U.S. 602, 614). For example, in *Lynch v. Donnelly* (1984) the Court held unconstitutional the state allowing a private organization to place a crèche in front of a public building, but *Allegheny v. ACLU* (1989) held constitutional the state paying to place a crèche in a public park. Each was constitutional or unconstitutional because of the context of the display.

The more intertwined the relationship between the two schools the more likely that the arrangement is unconstitutional (*Zellers v. Huff*, 1951). Hence, it would probably be unconstitutional for a secular "half-day" charter school to share a building with a religious school even if it were constitutional for a religiously-indoctrinating charter school to operate. The issue of entanglement is different than the issue of religious effect or advancement, even though entanglement is now generally considered an aspect of effect. If a separate foundation owned the building and then rented the building to the charter school and to the religious school it makes the relationship more likely to be constitutional. However, the constitutionality of the arrangement would depend on the particulars, such as whether the schools had the same employees and attendees and whether any religious objects were found in the rooms used by the charter school.

Even if the federal constitution allowed a charter school to share facilities with a religious school, it is possible that the state constitution would prohibit such an arrangement. States have addressed "shared space" programs with different results. Nebraska held that it was constitutional for a school district to lease classrooms from faith-based schools in order to provide needed special education services (*State of Nebraska ex rel. The School District Of Hartington v. Nebraska State Board of Education*, 1972). Illinois has also allowed a school district to operate an experimental program in which students attended both public and faith-based schools (*Morton, v. Board of Education of the City of Chicago*, 1966). The Oregon Court of Appeals, however, held that the state constitution prohibited programs in which a public school and faith-based school shared facilities (*Fisher v. Clackamas County School District 12*, 1973). Thus, it is possible that sharing facilities may be constitutional in some states, but not others.

SCHOOL OPERATED BY A RELIGIOUS ORGANIZATION

A group of parents approach their clergyman about opening a school. Parents feel that the local public school is not aware enough of the emotional needs of the students. They also fear that many of the other parents are not involved enough with their children. The parents want to create a school in which parents, teachers, and administrators better know the needs and sensibilities of the students. They approached their clergy because one of the parents read that religious schools are more successful at being aware of the needs and well-being of children.

The clergyman states that he will start a school, but it must have prayer and religion classes. He says that religion gives a school a sense of cohesion. The school is initially planned as a religious school. During the planning it becomes evident that many parents of different religions and many nonreligious parents are also interested in a school dedicated to the welfare of children. A compromise is reached: the school has prayer and religion classes, but they are optional. One general religion class, which is non-proselytizing, is mandatory. Approximately 60% of the children who attend the school go to the prayer and denominational classes.

The questions addressed by the final hypothetical charter school examine the inherent issues if a religious organization operated a charter school. These seven questions address the issue of whether a charter school can endorse religion or even proselytize. (1) Can a religious organization operate a charter school? (2) Can a charter school have religious criteria for admission? (3) To what extent can a religion class be taught in a charter school? (4) Can a charter school require religious instruction? (5) Can a charter school require religious exercises or worship? (6) Can a charter school identify with a denomination? (7) Can states exclude religious based charter schools from forming?

Can a Religious Organization Operate a Charter School?

The term religious organization is meant to include any organization with a religious mission. There is a spectrum of such organizations. A religious organization could, for example, operate a secular charter school as part of its mission to help children. Moreover, a church or synagogue or mosque would almost certainly create a separate nonprofit organization to operate a charter school. Some of the separate organizations would identify as religious and others would not, depending on the mission of the organization.

This issue is similar to coreligionists opening a charter school discussed earlier. In *Board of Education v. Grumet* (1994) the Supreme Court addressed the issue of a state statute fashioning a village of coreligionists into a school district for the secular purpose of providing the town's special-needs children with a free public education. As part of the Court's analysis it noted that the state could not through a specific act delegate civic authority to a religious leader (512 U.S. 687, 699). The Court found no constitutional difference between the delegating power to a group of coreligionists and delegating power to a religious leader or institution.

The *Grumet* (1994) decision, however, did not hold that the community could not constitutionally make up a school district, but merely held that the New York State act that made the town into a school district was unconstitutional because the act was directed toward adherents of a specific belief. The Court noted that a religiously homogenous group was not prevented from exercising civic authority when the authority was meted out on a neutral basis. Statutes are unconstitutional when they grant civic authority based on religious status.

It does not matter if the status is churches generally and or a specific community of religious adherents. The Court did not hold that a religious organization could never exercise civic authority, but merely that such organizations must exercise that authority based on religiously neutral statutes. That does not of course mean that all delegations of civic authority made to religious organizations would be constitutional. If a delegation required continual monitoring to ensure that the authority was exercised on a secular basis, then it would be unconstitutional (*Lemon v. Kurtzman*, 1971; *Walz v. Tax Com. of the City of New York*, 1970), as would a delegation that primarily benefited religious organizations (*Larkin v. Grendel's Den*, 1982).

Grumet (1994) helps us understand whether a charter school operated by a religious organization would have the effect of advancing religion, but does not answer the question whether such a school would necessarily unconstitutionally entangle church and state. *Lemon v. Kurtzman* (1971) found unconstitutional salary supplements given to teachers of secular subjects at private religious schools. The Court held that the constant monitoring of teachers to ensure that only secular subjects were taught (as was defined in the statute), would have the effect of impermissibly entangling the state with religion. In 1985, the Court used the monitoring principle to find unconstitutional two programs that paid teachers in private schools (*Aguilar v. Felton*, 1985; *Grand Rapids v. Ball*, 1985). In *Agostini v. Felton* (1997) the Court limited those rulings.

The *Agostini* (1997) Court rejected the principle that a state employee would feel compelled to integrate religion into secular classes taught on site at private religious schools. *Agostini*, however, was different from *Lemon* in two important respects. First, the program in *Agostini* applied to both public and private schools. Second, the teachers in *Agostini* were state employees paid by the state, while the teachers in *Lemon* (1971) were private employees given supplementary pay by the state. The teachers in *Lemon* had two masters, a secular one and a religious one. Consequently, the salary supplement program would still entangle church and state. However, *Lemon* does not resolve the question whether a religious organization operating a charter school would be considered as having two masters, the religious institution and the state, or just one.

Although *Agostini* (1997) and other cases indicate that the Court is more willing to trust that state employees will not inculcate religion, those cases are silent on the issue of private employees. It is unclear whether a charter school operated by a religious organization would necessitate the sort of monitoring that would be necessary to ensure that the state only funded the secular program. Thus far, charter schools have only been operated by secular organizations because state statutes have specifically excluded religious organizations from operating charter schools. If states begin to allow religious organizations to form charter schools, it is possible, but unlikely, that more religious charter schools would form than nonreligious ones.

The Supreme Court has prohibited the state from giving certain types of aid to private schools because the vast majority of private schools are religious (*Committee for Public Education and Religious Liberty v. Nyquist*, 1973; *Sloan v. Lemon*, 1973). The Court has, however, found constitutional aid that goes to both public and private schools (*Agostini v. Felton*, 1997; *Mueller v. Allen*, 1983). Similarly, without addressing issues of content, allowing charter schools to be operated by religious organizations would be constitutional, so long as the majority of charter schools remained secular. The mere fact that at some point in the future religious schools might come to dominate the numbers of charter schools would not be enough to void charters run by religious organizations. The Supreme Court has rejected the argument based on a mathematical analysis comparing the amounts claimed by public and private schooling parents because such an approach would not provide a principle by which to examine each incident.

This does not mean that a charter statute would necessarily survive if the majority of charters were consistently granted to religious organizations. The Court has never dealt with a benefit program that initially provided a benefit to a majority of secular organizations, but eventually aided a majority of religious organizations. It is likely that the nonfunding principle embodied in the *Lemon* (1971) test, which the Court still used in *Agostini* (1997), would nullify such an arrangement.

Because charter schools are public schools, but are operated by private individuals and organizations, the constitutionality of various types of religion-based schools is difficult to predict. One of most difficult predictions to make is whether a religious organization could operate a charter school. Although the dicta (nonbinding discussion) of the Court in *Grumet* (1994) indicates that a religious organization could operate a charter school, it is unclear whether such a school would cause an excessive entanglement between church and state.

If religiously-indoctrinating charter schools were constitutional (see below), then there would be no need to monitor the schools for religious content. However, if the curricula of schools operated by religious organizations were bound by the same Establishment Clause restrictions as public schools, then the state would likely have to monitor the charter school to ensure that the state's secular curriculum standards were met.

Can a Charter School Have Religious Criteria for Admission?

Religious criteria for admission are certainly unconstitutional. As discussed above, a public charter school cannot require that all teachers, administrators or board members profess a certain faith or belief in god (*Torcaso v. Watkins*, 1961). For example, in *Stark v. Independent School District, No. 640* (1997), the Eighth Circuit noted the importance of the fact that the "school is a public school open to all, and there is no evidence that any students wishing to attend there have been turned away" (123 F.3d 1068, 1074). While a charter school may accommodate the religious beliefs of its students and may by virtue of its design contain coreligionists, a charter school cannot require that student be of a particular faith to attend.

To What Extent Can a Religion Class be Taught in a Charter School?

In *Edwards v. Aguillard* (1987), the Supreme Court addressed a state statute that banned teaching the theory of evolution unless accompanied by instruction in creation science. The Court held that the statute was unconstitutional because it did not have a secular purpose. The Court noted the justification for close examination of state acts that implicate religion in schools.

> The Court has been particularly vigilant in monitoring compliance with the Establishment Clause in elementary and secondary schools. Families entrust public schools with the education of their children, but condition their trust on the understanding that the classroom will not purposely be used to advance religious views that may conflict with the private beliefs of the student and his or her family. Students in such institutions are impressionable and their attendance is involuntary. (482 U.S. 578, 583–84)

Religion can of course be taught without advancing religious viewpoints. Various lower courts have held that teaching about religion is constitutional (*Altman v. Bedford*, 1999). Moreover, the Free Exercise Clause does not require schools to allow children to opt out of lessons their parents find religiously objectionable (*Mozert v. Hawkins*, 1987).

Courses about the Bible, a religion, or different religions can be taught in public schools so long as the course does not endorse a religion or religion generally. Religious instruction in a charter school must not initiate students into a particular religious tradition (Thiessen, 1993, p. 4). If a charter school's board members, teachers, and students were primarily of the same faith, there would be a great danger that a course about that belief would endorse that faith or even attempt to initiate students into that religion. The issue is not the Bible itself, which is an appropriate book to study, but the selectivity, emphasis, objectivity, and interpretive manner in which the Bible is taught (*Wiley v. Franklin*, 1979).

A federal District Court in *Wiley v. Franklin* (1979) addressed a public school's course in the Bible. The court held that the administration had to create standards that would provide a nonreligious focus of the course. The same District Court later addressed the way the courses were taught. It examined actual classroom tapes and held that some instruction impermissibly conveyed a religious message while other lessons did not. The *Wiley* decisions illustrate the difficulty of creating a course about one's own religion that does not endorse that religion. It is significantly easier for a teacher to neutrally teach about Buddhism or the ancient religions of Mexico (*Altman v. Bedford*, 1999) than about her own religion (*Wiley v. Franklin*, 1980). Of course indoctrination can occur in both religious and secular subjects (Thiessen, 1993). Though the constitution only forbids religious indoctrination (*Doe v. Human*, 1989).

Courses about religion can be taught in charter schools; however, teachers must be vigilant about not endorsing the religion taught. It is highly unlikely that religion could be taught in a school that was operated by a religious organization without endorsing that organization's religion. A charter school can teach a course about religion so long as that course does not endorse (or denigrate) the religion being taught, but instead includes lessons that are literary or historical.

Can a Charter School Require Religious Instruction?

Whether a charter school can require religious instruction rests on the answer to two questions. First, the charter school must have the power to require such a course. Second, the Establishment Clause must not prohibit it.

Legislatures have plenary power over school curricula. It is well established that the legislature can require subjects be taught that are essential to good citizenship (*Pierce v. Society of Sisters*, 1925). The limits on the powers of the legislature have been defined in terms of what it cannot ban and what it cannot require. State legislatures cannot ban private schools (*Pierce v. Society of Sisters*) or regulate them out of existence (*Farrington v. Tokushige*, 1927). They cannot prohibit teaching foreign languages (*Meyer v. Nebraska*, 1923) or evolution (*Epperson v. Arkansas*, 1968). They also cannot require that creation science be taught if evolution is taught because such a rule does not advance academic freedom and has a religious purpose (*Edwards v. Aguillard*, 1987).

A legislature may delegate its remaining power to school boards or charter schools and often does. Moreover, if the legislature does not act by setting the curriculum, local school boards have extensive implied delegated powers (Reutter, 1994, p. 164). Lastly, school administrators exercise tremendous authority over the curriculum. School administrators, for example, can suppress student speech that is part of the curriculum so long as the action is "reasonably related to legitimate pedagogical concerns" (*Hazelwood Sch. Dist. v. Kuhlmeier*, 1988, 484 U.S. 260, 273).

In *Medeiros v. Kiyosaki* (1970), the Supreme Court of Hawaii addressed the question of whether the State Board of Education could include filmstrips on sex education as part of the fifth-and sixth-grade curriculum. Because parents could voluntarily withdraw their children from the lesson, they had no free exercise challenge to the course. Parents choose whether their child attends a particular charter school.

The reasoning in *Frost v. Hawkins County Board of Education* (1988), however, is more persuasive. There is no constitutional requirement that schools allow students to opt-out of lessons that are religiously or personally objectionable. The only time that a school must allow children to opt-out of a lesson or activity is when that activity requires the students to do an action that violates their religious beliefs (*West Virginia v. Barnette*, 1943). Consequently, the mandatory nature of the religion course would not make it unconstitutional.

The fact that a religion course can be mandatory does not mean that other constitutional requirements do not apply. As discussed earlier in this chapter under the heading "Can a charter school teach a course in the relationship between religion and morality?" a course in religion cannot espouse religious dogma (*Doe v. Human*, 1989). Any course must not have "the primary effect of advancing religion" (*Hall v. Board of School Commissioners of Conecuh County*, 1981, 656 F.2d 999, 1002). Teaching about religion is constitutional so long as the course does not endorse the religion taught regardless of whether it is mandatory.

Can a Charter School Require Religious Exercises or Worship?

As discussed above, a public school cannot endorse and certainly cannot coerce prayer or religious worship. Moreover, a string of cases in the 1960s held unconstitutional prayer or Bible readings over school loudspeakers or at assemblies (*Abington v. Schempp*, 1963; *Chamberlin v. Dade County*, 1964; *Engel v. Vitale*, 1962). A public school, including a charter school, cannot authorize prayer in any situation. Prayer must be wholly voluntary to students. Therefore a charter school cannot have required religious exercises or worship.

Students are of course free to engage in student-initiated religious exercises that do not materially and substantially interfere with the requirements of appropriate discipline in the operation of the school. It is unclear whether a school could require students to participate in a moment of silence. Although students whose religious beliefs prohibit them from attending moments of silence must be excused, whether a school could otherwise require attendance at a moment of silence is not apparent.

Can a Charter School Identify With a Denomination?

The issue of a charter school's identification with a denomination is similar to the issue of a religious organization running a charter school. A denominational school is not necessarily a school that is operated by a religious organization. By denomination I do not intend to exclude from analysis "Christian" or "Protestant" schools (Feldman, 1997, pp. 2-3). I use the term denomination to distinguish this hypothetical school from schools that support or teach morality or religiosity generally. There is a spectrum of what denominational means, from a school with a token affiliation to a school that is perversely sectarian. A private organization could operate a denominational charter school for profit. A religious organization could as part of its mission operate a secular school.

Affiliation with a denomination is certainly not limited to schools operated by churches, especially since most religious organizations would form a separate nonprofit organization to operate a charter school, or even a private school. Affiliation occurs when a school identifies itself with a denomination or a religion. For example a "Jewish" school is probably not operated by a synagogue, yet it calls itself Jewish and may (or may not) affiliate with a Jewish accreditation body.

A charter school may associate with a denomination in any number of ways. An otherwise secular charter school may choose to be qualified through a religiously affiliated accreditation body. A charter school may partner with a church to provide extra curricular activities. A charter school may join a religious sports league. The religious display cases decided by the Supreme Court illustrate that the context of a religious activity often determines its constitutionality (*County of Allegheny v. ACLU*, 1989; *Lynch v. Donnelly*, 1984).

Joining a religious sports league on its own may not endorse a religion, but that in addition to other activities may constitute endorsing religion (*Roberts v. Madigan*, 1990). Affiliation with a denomination in the context of this question, however, refers to a school that identifies itself as religious. Up until now various religious activities have been addressed. This section addresses whether a charter school may hold itself out as a religious school.

The issue of monitoring a religiously affiliated charter school is in many ways different from the issue of monitoring a charter school that is operated by a religious organization. The monitoring of a secular charter school formed by a religious organization is done to ensure that the program is not religious. Once the school's program is assumed to be religious, however, there is no need for such monitoring—the program is either unconstitutional because it has a denomination or is constitutional in spite of it. The only issue of monitoring would be examining whether the secular and religious programs were funded separately, as the Constitution requires (*Committee for Public Education v. Regan*, 1980).

The Constitution clearly prohibits a public school from maintaining a denomination. Public schools and public school teachers cannot endorse religion. Public schools are prohibited from including nondenominational prayer at graduation (*Lee v. Weisman*, 1992). Denominational prayer is obviously a greater constitutional threat. Lower courts have held various denominational activities unconstitutional. Schools cannot post pictures of Jesus (*Washegesic v. Bloomingdale*, 1993). Teachers cannot place religious posters on their classroom walls or keep the Bible on their desks (*Roberts v. Madigan*, 1990). Teachers cannot conduct classroom activities that are inherently religious even when those activities have a secular purpose (*Altman v. Bedford*, 1999).

Another means of analysis that could be applied parallels the analysis that the Supreme Court has done in the case of private religious colleges. The Court has held that state aid to private religious colleges does not create the same Establishment Clause violation as state aid to private religious elementary and secondary schools. The Court has articulated four reasons for the difference. Because college students are older, they are less subject to religious indoctrination. College courses are less subject to sectarian influence. Church-owned colleges maintain a high degree of academic freedom (*Tilton v. Richardson*, 1971). Finally, religious colleges are a smaller percentage of the schools receiving the aid (*Roemer v. Maryland*, 1976).

Because of these factors, the Court has examined aid to private colleges on a school-by-school basis, rather than examining an aid statute as a whole. Aid to private religious colleges is allowed so long as the college is not pervasively sectarian. Charter schools could be subjected to this level of analysis, rather than courts assuming that a denominational charter is pervasively sectarian and thus unconstitutional. The analysis would depend upon the academic freedom of the teachers and the relationship between the curriculum and the controlling body. However, because of the age of students, it is unlikely that the courts would use this analysis. Additionally parents may want to form a charter school that is not merely denominational, but pervasively sectarian.

Whether a charter school can be affiliated with a denomination is closely related to whether a charter school is a state actor. If charter schools are state actors then charter schools certainly cannot subscribe to a denomination. If charter schools are not state actors, then it is very likely that they can subscribe to a denomination. In deciding public school cases, courts always assume the schools are subject to constitutional limitations because, as public schools, they are government actors

(Goldstein, 1998, p. 134). However, charter schools are in many ways distinct from traditional public schools and may not be state actors.

If charter schools were subject to constitutional limitations, the Establishment Clause surely would prohibit them from maintaining a denomination. The Constitution, with the exception of the 13th Amendment, only applies to the state and to state actors. Thus, whether a charter school may maintain a denomination is essentially whether charter schools are state actors.

Whether charter schools are state actors is a complex question. Since most states consider charter schools to be public schools, the Establishment Clause applies to them. Because the Establishment Clause prohibits the state's endorsement of religion, denominational charter schools would violate the Constitution. Moreover, if denominational charter schools were constitutional, they could have required religious exercises, prayers, and religion classes.

States have a great deal of power in legislatively defining whether charter schools are public or private schools and states have thus far defined charter schools as public schools. The states' power is not how they label charter schools, but rather how states structurally define charters. Moreover, several states have constitutional provisions that provide that state funding for education must only go to public schools (Goldstein, 1998, p. 153).

Some state constitutions require that public schools must be maintained by the state. Because the chartering process, the degree of autonomy, and the relationship between the state and the charter school varies, it is impossible to state definitively that charter schools are or are not state actors. Michigan at one point held its charter statute unconstitutional because in that state, a public school must be under the exclusive control of the state and open to all children in the school district (*Parachoid v. Governor of Michigan*, 1996). The statue was subsequently amended to allow charters to form. Charter schools obviously have some characteristics of state agencies and other characteristics of private organizations. These characteristics vary from state to state based on the regulatory process of creating and monitoring charter schools.

Whether charter schools are state actors will have to be decided on a state-by-state basis. Michigan, for example, has also decided that charter schools are state actors for the purpose of the state constitution (*Council v. Michigan*, 1997). Because constitutional standards vary between state and federal constitutions, it is also possible for charter schools of a state to be considered state actors for the purposes of the state constitution, but not the federal Constitution, or vice versa. However, it is most likely that a charter school in any state will either be considered a state actor or not under both the state and federal constitutions.

The current Michigan charter law specifically defines charter schools as public schools. "A public school academy is a public school under [the Michigan] state constitution" (Mich. Comp. Laws Ann. ["MCLA], 2004, § 380.501) Charter schools, however, are organized under the Michigan nonprofit corporation act. Interestingly, Michigan only excludes religion based charter schools to the extent required by the state or federal constitution (MCLA § 380.502). Michigan charter schools also must comply with federal laws that apply to public bodies or school districts and maintain admissions policies and collective bargaining agreements that are equivalent to public schools.

Whether a charter school is a state actor presents a different type of inquiry from the previous questions because this question has much greater implications and applies to all charters in a state whether religion-based or not. Consequently, a number of relevant issues must be addressed. The Supreme Court has generally examined the issue of religious acts by public schools in the context of state or district policy. For example, *Stone v. Graham* (1980) invalidated a Kentucky statute requiring that all public schools post the Ten Commandments in every classroom in the state. However, the Court has been clear that any state act with a religious purpose is unconstitutional (*McCreary County v. ACLU*, 2005). *McCreary County* held unconstitutional displays that included the Ten Commandments in county courthouses.

The posting of the Ten Commandments in all schools is a very different action qualitatively by the state than a single school posting the Ten Commandments in its halls. Similarly, in most of the daily prayer, Bible readings, and moment of silence cases, the Court addressed state statutes requiring the daily devotions in all schools, or state statutes encouraging or permitting them in all schools. However, courts have treated actions by a single school, even acts by a single teacher, to the same standard. The recent Supreme Court cases addressing the constitutionality of Ten Commandments displays are also premised on the history, context and purposes of those displays (*McCreary County, Ky. v. American Civil Liberties Union of Ky.*, 2005; *Van Orden v. Perry*, 2005).

In *Lee v. Weisman* (1992) the Supreme Court held unconstitutional a principal's inviting a Rabbi to speak at a high school graduation. Justice Kennedy wrote for the Court that an invocation by a member of the clergy at a graduation would be religious coercion. It is of course easy to argue that when the state requires all schools to carry out a religious action, that the act will constitute and endorsement of that action by the state. It is often apparent whether the state legislators were motivated by religious sentiment and whether the action has the effect of advancing (or endorsing) religion. The religious display cases have also been decided examining the context of the individual display (*County of Allegheny v. ACLU*,

1989; *Capitol Square Advisory Board v. Pinette*, 1995; *Lynch v. Donnelly*, 1984; *McCreary County v. ACLU*, 2005; *Van Orden v. Perry*, 2005). Lower courts, however, have generally interpreted the Supreme Court's religion jurisprudence in school cases as meaning that an individual school cannot do what the state (or school district) cannot do generally (*Washegesic v. Bloomingdale*, 1993). Lower courts have also held that public school teachers cannot commit acts that endorse religion in their classroom (*Altman v. Bedford*, 1999; *Roberts v. Madigan*, 1990).

Because states have thus far created charter schools as public schools, they will be treated as public schools in the eyes of the Constitution. The Supreme Court (or any court) is very likely to hold religious schools funded through a per-capita aid program, like charter schools, unconstitutional. As public schools, charter schools would have to satisfy all the constitutional requirements of public school. Thus, a religiously indoctrinating charter school would be unconstitutional.

The Supreme Court has addressed when a private agency is a state actor. In *Rendell-Baker v. Kohn* (1982), the Supreme Court held that private schools, no matter how regulated and no matter how funded, were not state actors according to the U.S. Constitution. "A state normally can be held responsible for a private decision only when it has exercised coercive power or has provided such significant encouragement, either overt or covert, that the choice must in law be deemed to be that of the state" (*Rendell-Baker v. Kohn*, 457 U.S. 830, 840). Thus, private schools are not state actors. "That a private entity performs a function which serves the public does not make its acts state action" (*Rendell-Baker v. Kohn*, 457 U.S. 830, 840). Charter schools, however, are not private schools; they are public schools. Thus, it is likely that most states' charter schools would be considered state actors.

The Supreme Court defines a state actor as when the state provides significant encouragement either overt or covert, or when the private actor operates as a willful participant in joint activity with the State or its agents (*Brentwood v. Tennessee Secondary School Athletic Assoc.*, 2001). A nominally private entity is a state actor when it is controlled by an agency of the state, when it has been delegated a public function of the state, when it is entwined with governmental policies, or when government is entwined with its management or control (*Brentwood v. Tennessee Secondary School Athletic Assoc.*).

More simply, "Is the alleged infringement of federal rights fairly attributable to the state" (*Rendell-Baker v. Kohn*, 1982, 457 U.S. 830, 840)? Mere regulation and funding by the state is not enough to hold a private actor a state actor. Charter schools would probably qualify as "a willful participant in joint activity with the State" (*Rendell-Baker v. Kohn*, 457 U.S. 830, 840).

The charter school contracts with the state or district to operate a public school.

The key question is likely to be whether the charter school has been "delegated a public function of the state." *Rendell-Baker* (1982) holds that all schools are not state actors, even though education is a public function. Being a public function is not enough by itself, the question is whether the function performed has been "traditionally the exclusive prerogative of the State." Although education has certainly not traditionally been the exclusive prerogative of the state, *public* education has been the exclusive prerogative of the state and thus charter schools are most likely to be held to be state actors. Moreover, many state constitutions specifically define charter schools as public schools and specifically define public education as a state function (Goldstein, 1998; e.g., Mich. Comp. Laws Ann., 2004, § 380.501). Charter schools also function very much like traditional public schools with regard to open admission, ultimate government control, and so forth.

Although it is very likely that courts will hold charter schools to be state actors, the argument that charter schools are not state actors is not unreasonable. If charter schools were not state actors, then no federal constitutional requirements would apply to them. The only issue would be whether charter schools are private-choice programs or per-capita aid programs (*Mitchell v. Helms*, 2000). A private-aid program is constitutional because when the government provides aid directly to the student beneficiary the student retains control over whether the government aid will be applied toward a religious education. Because of the way charter schools are funded, however, they would probably be considered per-capita aid programs and therefore a pervasively religious charter school could not be funded by the state.

States also could not purposely draft a charter statute in order to encourage the formation of religious schools. Such a statute would violate the Establishment Clause, specifically the purpose prong of the *Lemon* (1971) test. For example, it is well established that it is unconstitutional for a school board to attempt to legislate around a desegregation order through a voucher program (*Griffin v. County School Board*, 1964). The state may not operate schools in some districts but not others in order to avoid constitutional requirements. Similarly, a state could not institute a voucher or charter system drafted to avoid the requirements of the Establishment Clause.

Even if charter schools were not considered state actors, many states have enacted versions of the nineteenth century Blaine Amendment. The Blaine amendment stated:

> No money raised by taxation in any State, for the support of public schools, or derived from any public fund therefor, nor any public lands devoted thereto, shall ever be under the control of any religious sect, nor shall any money so raised, or lands so devoted be divided between religious sects or denominations. (*Congressional Record*, 44th Congress, 1st session, 14 December, 1875, quoted in, Pfeffer, 1967, p. 146)

Although Congress did not pass the Blaine amendment, as of 2003 37 states had provisions in their constitutions that prohibit state monies from funding religious schools (The Becket Fund for Religious Liberty, 2003). Consequently, even if denominational charters were constitutional, many state constitutions would prohibit them.

Charter schools are bound by federal constitutional requirements, including the separation between church and state. Because charter schools are probably state actors under the law, a charter school cannot identify with a denomination nor can one be pervasively sectarian. Moreover, even if charter schools were not state actors, constitutional restrictions would still apply: because of the way they are funded, as per-capita aid programs, a pervasively religious or denominational charter school probably could not constitutionally be funded by the state.

Can States Exclude Religion-Based Charter Schools From Forming?

Whether states can prevent parents from forming religion-based charter schools is a substantially different question from the others presented. The previous questions have all assumed the state voluntarily allowed a religion-based charter school to form and addressed what forms the Establishment Clause permitted those schools to take. Whether the state has the power to exclude religious organizations from operating charter schools is substantially different.

Most issues involving the separation between church and state can be divided into three categories: what the state cannot do, what the state can or may do, and what the state must do. The state cannot sponsor or encourage prayer (*Santa Fe v. Doe*, 2000). The state may provide loans of secular materials to faith-based schools (*Mitchell v. Helms*, 2000). The state must allow students to opt out of activities that violate their religion (*West Virginia v. Barnette*, 1943). Thus far, this work has dealt with the first two and now we begin an analysis within the final category.

The Supreme Court has never held that the Establishment Clause or the Free Exercise Clause required that aid go to a religious institution or a person attending such an institution (*Locke v. Davey*, 2004). In all cases where the state was required to provide aid to a religious organization or person attending a religious institution, that aid was based on a statute or other right, for example, Individuals With Disabilities Education Act (*Zobrest v. Catalina Foothills*, 1993), Equal Access Act (*Board of Education v. Mergens*, 1990), state statute providing assistance to the blind (*Witters v. Washington*, 1986).

The strongest support for the argument that the state must allow religious charter schools to form is based on the language of the Court's access cases, *Widmar v. Vincent* (1981), *Lamb's Chapel v. Center Moriches* (1993), *Rosenberger v. University of Virginia* (1995), and *Good News Club v. Milford Central School* (2001). In each of those cases, a state actor (a school or college) allowed groups to use its facilities or provided some neutral benefit. In each case, the state actor denied the benefit to a religious organization that fit the nonreligious requirements of the benefit. In all four cases, the Supreme Court held that the state could not deny access to the religious organization. In all of these cases, however, the organization's right to access was protected by the Free Speech Clause, not the Establishment Clause or the Free Exercise Clause. Therefore, the right to use the facilities was not based on the religious viewpoint, but rather in spite of it. I.e., the exclusion could not be justified by the religious viewpoint.

In each of the access cases, the state actor, either a school, school district, or university, created a forum for expression (called a limited public forum or a designated public forum), excluded religious speech from that forum, and could not justify a particular exclusion on the basis of the Establishment Clause. When a state creates a forum, two different standards apply. When the state excludes a speaker on the basis of the viewpoint, it must justify that exclusion with a compelling state interest (*Perry Education Assoc. v. Perry Local Educators' Assoc.*, 1983). The state, however, may make topic, time, place, or manner exclusions that are reasonable. Exclusions based on the topic are often referred to as content exclusions. For the sake of clarity, I will avoid the word "content" because courts often refer to exclusions based on viewpoint as "substantive content" exclusions.

In *Widmar v. Vincent* (1981), a state university denied access to a registered student group on the basis of a university regulation that prohibited use of buildings "for purposes of religious worship or religious teaching" (454 U.S. 263, 265). Because the university had created a forum generally open to student groups, the university had to justify the denial of access according to the standard of the Free Speech Clause. The university attempted to justify the exclusion based on the Establishment Clause, but that argument was rejected.

Similarly, in *Lamb's Chapel v. Center Moriches* (1993), a school district denied a request by a church to use school facilities after school to show a film about family values and child rearing. The school district had opened a forum by allowing other groups to use the school building after school hours. The school had a rule prohibiting the use of the premises for religious purposes. The Supreme Court held that the exclusion could not be justified by the rule because the topic of the presentation was not religion, but was child rearing and family values from a religious viewpoint. The Court held that the exclusion could not be based on the Establishment Clause.

In *Rosenberger v. University of Virginia* (1995), a state university created a fund for student groups to pay for publication costs. A Christian student group was denied funding because its publication was religious. The university justified the denial based on a rule against funding religious activity and the Establishment Clause. The Court held that because the student group fit the neutral criteria for funding their publication, the publication was protected by the Free Speech Clause. Once again, the Establishment Clause did not justify denying the funds.

In *Good News Club v. Milford Central School* (2001), a school board banned a private Christian organization from operating an after-school program in its facilities even though the school permitted the school to be used for "social, civic, recreational, and entertainment uses pertaining to the community welfare." Banning the club was unconstitutional because the Club sought "to address a subject otherwise permitted under the rule, the teaching of morals and character, from a religious standpoint" (533 U.S. 98, 109).

The Free Speech Clause allows the state to exclude the topic of religion from a limited public forum, but the state cannot exclude a religious viewpoint. *Lamb's Chapel* most clearly illustrates the distinction between the topic of religion and the religious viewpoint. The presentation was about family values and child rearing, not about religion. Consequently, the exclusion was improperly based on the religious viewpoint of the presentation, not the topic of religion. In *Rosenberger* (1995), having allowed other student newspapers to publish articles about religion, the university could not exclude this topic, and could not prevent students from writing about religion from a religious viewpoint.

Locke v. Davey (2004) illustrates the importance of proving that the state established a public forum. The student who was denied a scholarship on the basis of his pursuing a theology degree was not able to prove that Washington State had created such a forum and was therefore limited to a Free Exercise Clause claim, which was rejected by the Supreme Court.

If states were required to allow religion-based charters to form, three things would have to be true. First, the state must have created a limited public forum when it created the charter school system. Second, the prohibition against religious charters must be viewpoint discrimination in violation against the Free Speech Clause. Third, the Establishment Clause cannot justify the prohibition.

Two lower court decisions have analyzed similar arguments in the context of education, *Columbia Union College v. Clarke* (1998) and *Bagley v. Raymond* (1999). In *Columbia Union College*, the school argued that *Rosenberger* required the state to fund religious colleges under a state program that gave grants to public and private colleges. The funding program was the same one at issue in the Supreme Court case *Roemer v. Maryland* (1976), which had held distributions to religious colleges constitutional, so long as the colleges were not pervasively religious.

Columbia Union College argued that the state had created a forum and could not deny the grants to the college based on its religious viewpoint even if the school was pervasively religious. The Fourth Circuit held that by creating the grant program, the state was funding the speech of colleges and that the denial had to be justified based on the Establishment Clause to be constitutional. The Fourth Circuit Court of Appeals went on to hold that the Supreme Court had not overruled *Roemer v. Maryland* (1976) and that denying of funds would be constitutional if the college was pervasively religious.

By contrast, in *Bagley v. Raymond* (1999) the Supreme Court of Maine addressed whether religious schools could constitutionally be excluded from voucher programs. The U.S. Supreme Court subsequently in *Zelman* (2002) addressed whether states can create voucher programs that **can** be used at a religious school, not whether when vouchers having been enacted **must** be usable at religious schools. The Maine Supreme Court wholly rejected the argument based on *Rosenberger* (1995) and the other forum cases.

> The issue before us is wholly distinct from those cases. The parents cannot assert that they have been denied a forum for any type of speech. Rather, they seek to have the State pay for their children's education. Moreover, the *Rosenberger* Court explicitly distinguished school aid cases when it noted that "this case is not controlled by the principle that special Establishment Clause dangers exist where government makes direct money payments to sectarian institutions.... It is undisputed that no public funds flow directly into [the religious group's] coffers under the program at issue." (728 A.2d 127, 146-47)

These two lower courts thus interpret the scope of *Rosenberger* (1995) differently. Although they come to similar conclusions, denying funding the *Columbia Union College* (1998) court equates money with speech, but the *Bagley* (1999) court does not. The approach of the *Bagley* court seems more in line with the Supreme Court's other opinions. To hold that any government aid is a forum supporting speech would radically change the scope of the Free Speech Clause.

The state creating a forum and the state providing aid are significantly different acts. Although the Court in *Rosenberger* (1995) refused to distinguish between access to facilities and funding, the funding in *Rosenberger* was directly related to speech; the students were publishing a newspaper. To hold that the funding of any educational enterprise constitutes the funding of speech would equate education as a right with speech. The Supreme Court, however, has rejected the argument that education is a fundamental right (*San Antonio v. Rodriguez*, 1973).

Is charter school legislation different from other aid programs? Does charter legislation open a limited public forum? This question is complex because one of the reasons for creating charter schools is to allow schools with distinctive characters to form. Additionally, some states may draft charter legislation in order to create a public forum, focusing on charter schools' missions, while other states might see charters as a funding mechanism, or means to reform education generally. Thus, state charter statutes will have to be examined individually to see if states have created a limited public forum.

As a general matter, charter schools are not a limited public forum. For example, the Michigan charter statute is silent regarding this purpose in creating "public school academies;" however, one of the items a school must place in its contract is "the purposes" for the proposed school (Mich. Comp. Laws Ann. § 380.502 (3) (c) (ii), 2004). This is probably not enough to create a limited public forum.

If a state has created a limited public forum, the exclusion of religion-based charter schools would be unconstitutional viewpoint discrimination. The denial of the charter would be on the basis of the religious viewpoint of the authors of the charter application. Of course, the state can exclude topics from being taught in charter schools. The state can require that no charter school teach religion, which would not discriminate on the basis of viewpoint. Excluding a topic is a classic permitted restriction on speech, which is constitutional so long as it is reasonable. A ban on teaching religion in charters might, however, violate the principles articulated in *Meyer v. Nebraska* (1923), which held that the state could not ban the teaching of German in all schools. *Meyer*, however, did not address the state's ability to regulate the curriculum in state-supported schools, but rather in private schools.

Can the establishment clause justify banning religion-based charters. Obviously the state cannot be forced to support a school that it could not allow to form. Thus, even if the state created a limited public forum, it could ban charter schools that violate the Establishment Clause, while it would have to allow other religion-based charter schools to form. Therefore, it is almost certainly the case that charter schools that identify with a denomination and hold themselves out as religious can be banned by the state.

Lastly, the Establishment Clause limitation may outweigh the Free Speech right since funding a school is a far more substantial state action than funding a newspaper or allowing an organization to use school facilities. It is, therefore, highly doubtful that the constitution requires that states must allow religious charters to form.

A more difficult question is posed by the possibility of parents who, for religious motivations, form an otherwise secular school. A variation on this question is whether parents could form a Jewish culture school or a Hindu culture school, or a Serbian culture school that addressed the Serbian Orthodox religion, or a school that promotes "African, Asian and Middle Eastern" culture and accommodates Islam. The line between religion and culture is not always clear. These charters would be accepted or denied and protected or banned based on their particulars, whether the school offered prayer, taught religious books, had admissions requirements, etc.

Variations on this scenario are presented in the first two hypotheticals. Assuming that the Establishment Clause does not ban such a school, the access cases present a powerful argument that the state could not deny the charter solely based on parents' religious motivations. In *Perry v. Milwaukee Public Schools* (2001), however, the Seventh Circuit Court of Appeals rejected the argument that denial of a charter school application on the basis of religious belief presented a constitutional claim. The case has very little value as precedent because it is a short unpublished order. Moreover, the plaintiff in that case had filed numerous frivolous complaints that "contain[ed] allegations so bizarre, rambling, and disjointed as to defy interpretation" (12 Fed. Appx. 406, 406). It is also unclear whether the charter that was denied in *Perry* was secular.

Although recent cases do not guarantee that denying a charter based on religious motivation would be unconstitutional, it seems possible that such a denial of an otherwise secular charter school would be unconstitutional viewpoint discrimination. The outcome would likely depend on whether a court accepted the argument that opening a charter school with a certain mission was an expression of free speech.

CHAPTER 5

SUMMARY AND CONCLUSIONS

THE CONTEXT OF RELIGION-BASED CHARTER SCHOOLS

Charter schools are public schools that are not part of a school district. The chartering organization has an agreement directly with the state (or other chartering agency) to operate the school under certain guidelines. The guiding principle of the charter school movement is accountability for autonomy, that is, making schools accountable and giving them more autonomy should increase achievement ("Charter School," 1998; Finn, Manno, & Vanourek, 2000, p. 14). Charter schools are accountable because they can be closed by the state if they do not meet performance criteria (Herszenhorn, 2004).

Charter schools are autonomous because they are not operated by a district and are often regulated much less than other public schools. By making the charter school, rather than the district, the unit of management, public school education naturally becomes more responsive to parental needs (Hill, Guthrie, & Pierce, 1997). This responsiveness would likely lead to a greater understanding and accommodation of parents' and students' religious needs.

It is overly simple to answer the question whether religion-based charter schools are constitutional with an obvious "no." A school can be religion-based without being a traditional religious school. As discussed in

Religious Charter Schools: Legalities and Practicalites, pp. 137–149
Copyright © 2007 by Information Age Publishing
All rights of reproduction in any form reserved.

chapter one, a religion-based charter school could take many forms, ranging from a school operated to provide convenient scheduling for afterschool religious classes, to a school that provides a room for students in which to pray, to a school that refrains from teaching lessons that parents find objectionable on religious grounds.

Charter schools present a vision of public education that is radically different from the current model of uniformity among public schools. The charter model of public schools is based on the uniqueness of school, defined in terms of autonomy and mission. This model tilts the state-parent educational power balance toward the parent by allowing families to form smaller charter schools that meet their specific needs rather than forming larger public schools that meet the district's general needs.

The Supreme Court's case law defining the appropriate role of religion in public schools, as discussed more fully in chapter 2, has left the situation murky and haphazard. In addition to the Supreme Court's own statement that the "wall of separation" is a "blurred, indistinct and variable barrier" (*Lemon v. Kurtzman*, 1971), the place of religion in school is often defined by a principal's personal views. This happens both when the principal is seemingly antagonistic toward religion—removing the Bible from the school library (*Roberts v. Madigan*, 1990)—and overly deferential toward students' religious beliefs—encouraging student-led prayer to circumnavigate a court order (*Chandler v. James*, 1997). Policies providing for charter schools, however, actively support the right of parents to direct their children's education more than they support any particular religious rights.

The Establishment Clause requires that the state be neutral toward religion. Justices on the Supreme Court, however, have not managed to agree about what the neutrality of a statute actually means. *Mitchell v. Helms*, which was discussed in great depth in chapter two, addressed the issue of the state loaning secular materials (maps, books, and so forth) to religious schools. The Justices had three different views on the constitutionality of such aid. The conservative faction believed that state aid could actually be diverted to religious purposes. The moderate faction held that aid can be divertible, but cannot actually be diverted to religious purposes. The liberal faction thought that state aid to religious schools couldn't be divertible to religious purposes.

The only thing that the three factions agreed upon was that state aid that cannot be diverted to religious purposes is constitutional. All the opinions, however, defined their positions as neutral toward religion. What is a neutral materials loan program? Is the neutrality of the program based on the general secular nature of the materials? Based on the secular use of the materials? Or based on proof that the materials can only be used for secular purposes?

Religion-based charter schools pose unique questions of law that will undoubtedly plague the courts for many years to come. The recent Supreme Court case involving vouchers (*Zelman v. Simmons-Harris*, 2002) could only indicate the Court's predisposition. But, because vouchers and charters are fundamentally different funding mechanisms, the constitutionality or unconstitutionality of one will not necessarily decide the other.

Religion-based charter schools are nearly inevitable as charter schools become more common. Some states may allow them as they allowed religious schools to participate in voucher programs. Religious parents will likely demand them. And religious organizations are likely to draft narrowly tailored charters to get around laws that ban them. This work has attempted to propound answers for the most common questions raised by the prospect of religion-based charter schools.

QUESTIONS ANSWERED BY
THE THREE HYPOTHETICAL SITUATIONS

Chapter four was a detailed examination of the issues facing religion-based charter schools. That chapter examined three hypothetical charter schools and the legal questions those schools pose. The three hypothetical situations considered: (1) a morally-based school founded by coreligionists, which forms because parents are unhappy with the values taught in public school; (2) a half-time secular school that exists to provide a non-controversial secular education to children who attend religious school every day; and (3) a traditional religious school operated by a religious organization. Each hypothetical situation was described and then each question related to that hypothetical was answered individually. This section summarizes those findings.

MORALLY-BASED SCHOOL FOUNDED BY CORELIGIONISTS

The seven questions addressed by the morally-based school generally addressed the issues of formation, mission, and control over the staff. Those questions are the following: (1) Can coreligionists form a charter school? (2) Can morality-based general propositions of good be taught in a charter school? (3) Can a charter school teach values espoused by coreligionists? (4) Can a charter school teach a course in the relationship between religion and morality? (5) Can a charter school have religious criteria for staff? (6) Can a charter school limit a teacher's right to express different worldviews? (7) Can a charter school offer optional prayer?

Coreligionists Can Form a Charter School

The right of coreligionists to form a charter school is protected by the constitution. Thus, the state cannot ban coreligionists from forming charter schools. The Establishment Clause prohibits the state from favoring a charter school founded by coreligionists over other charter schools.

Morality-Based General Propositions of Good Can Sometimes be Taught in a Charter School

Teaching about values, like teaching about religion, is constitutional. The permissibility of teaching values that coincide with religious beliefs depends upon the context of the lesson. Teaching values that are based on religious beliefs is constitutional so long as the lesson does not endorse religion.

A Charter School Probably Can Teach Values Espoused by Coreligionists

Values are a natural part of the educational process. The combination of coreligionists and a curriculum based on religious values probably would not, absent other factors, create an unconstitutional situation. A charter school is a single school teaching values espoused by coreligionists, posing a less significant constitutional problem than a district-wide values curriculum. However, a court would probably examine the values curriculum of a school run by coreligionists more closely than another charter school's similar curriculum.

A Charter School Can Teach a Course in the Relationship Between Religion and Morality if it is not From a Religious Viewpoint

Teaching about religion is constitutional so long as the religion taught is not endorsed by the lesson. A course that surveyed religions for the purpose of finding universal values would certainly be constitutional. The Bible is an appropriate subject in school, so long as the religious viewpoint of the Bible is not endorsed; that is, the course must teach about the Bible, not promote the Bible as truth. Although teaching about religion is permissible, teachers may not include activities that are inherently religious.

Charter Schools Cannot Have Religious Criteria for Staff

Charter schools cannot have religious criteria for staff. Charter schools are able to have religiously neutral behavior criteria for staff that do not impinge on the staff's freedom of speech. If charter schools were held to be private rather than public entities (i.e., nonstate actors), and the constitution allowed denominational charters to form, it is still not clear whether federal law would permit charter schools to have religious criteria for staff.

A Charter School Can Limit a Teacher's Right to Express Different Worldviews While on School Grounds

Charter school administrators may limit a teacher's expression so long as their actions are "reasonably related to legitimate pedagogical concerns" (*Miles v. Denver Public Schools*, 1991, 944 F.2d 773, 775). Although teachers have the right to free speech, school administrators have wide latitude for controlling that speech while teachers are on school grounds and when making hiring decisions. Therefore, a charter school may require that a teacher express the worldview of the charter while in school. Off school premises, however, a teacher has her full free speech protections and a school cannot legitimately prevent her from expressing her viewpoints when not in school, absent extreme circumstances.

Charter Schools Can Offer Students a Place to Pray

School-sponsored prayer is unconstitutional. Student-initiated prayer is sometimes protected by the constitution. Schools can provide rooms to students who want to pray during school hours, so long as the prayers are student-led and voluntary and rooms are available for all faiths and ideologies.

HALF-TIME SECULAR SCHOOL

The format of the section describing the half-time school differed from the other two hypothetical situations because it discussed two Supreme Court cases, *McCollum v. Illinois* (1948) and *Zorach v. Clauson* (1952), in depth. This section examined the issues of clergymen and religious organizations involvement in a charter's formation and operation. Those questions were: (1) Can a charter school form for the purpose of allowing students' ease of access to religious education? (2) Can a charter school form to provide students, who would otherwise attend religious schools, with a free, secular public education? (3) Can clergy sit on the board of a charter school? (4) Can a charter school share facilities with a religious school?

A Charter School Can Accommodate its Schedule to Enable Students to Attend Religious Activities After School

A charter school is free to set whatever school day hours it wishes, so long as it otherwise conforms to state regulations. A charter school could certainly require students to attend enriching after-school activities. A charter school could probably constitutionally form with the purpose of requiring students to attend after-school religious school. However, it seems very unlikely that a school would expressly place such a requirement in its charter when a similar secular reason is readily available.

A Charter School Can Form With the Purpose of Providing a Free Secular Education to Religious Students

Charter schools form using a religiously-neutral enabling statute. Consequently, any benefit to religious groups is not intended nor is it the primary purpose of the charter statute. Even though the intention of the school founders may be partly religious, their intent is not problematic in this instance since the school only provides a secular education. Charter schools, therefore, can form with the purpose of providing free secular education to religious students.

Clergy Can sit on the Board of a Charter School

The right of members of the clergy to sit on the board of a charter school is protected by the constitution, just as the right of atheists is so protected. Charters must be silent as to religious qualifications in terms of board membership. Clergy can also sit on the committees that apply for charters.

A Charter School's Ability to Share Facilities With a Faith-Based School Would Depend on the Nature of the Relationship Between the Schools

The Supreme Court has abandoned the proposition that a public employee on the grounds of a religious school will inevitably inculcate religion. The primary obstacle to a religious school and a charter school sharing facilities is the risk of creating a symbolic union between the two schools and thus between church and state. A charter school is of course free to rent out its facilities during the time children aren't in school. Several public schools have such a relationship with religious schools. If the schools were entirely separate, have substantially different students, and entirely different faculty, the sharing situation would probably be constitutional.

THE FULL-TIME RELIGIOUS SCHOOL WITH OPTIONAL PRAYER AND RELIGIOUS CLASSES

The final abstract charter school addressed the difficulties inherent when a charter school is operated by a religious organization. These seven questions addressed the of whether a charter school can endorse religion or even proselytize. (1) Can a religious organization operate a charter school? (2) Can a charter school have religious criteria for admission? (3) To what extent can a religion class be taught in a charter school? (4) Can a charter school require religious instruction? (5) Can a charter school require religious exercises or worship? (6) Can a charter school identify with a denomination? (7) Can states exclude religion-based charter schools from forming?

It is Unclear Whether a Religious Organization Can Operate a Charter School

The state certainly cannot delegate civic authority to a religious entity. Although the Supreme Court's nonfunding principle of the 1970s has been diminished, even the most conservative wing of the Court has always held that certain benefits may not go to religious organizations. Aid that is generally available and based on religiously neutral criteria, however, is usually constitutional. Although recent cases eliminated the Court's mistrust of state employees when they enter religious schools' grounds, the decision did not address the issue of religious organizations operating a public school.

Charter Schools Cannot Have Religious Criteria for Admission

A charter school cannot have religious criteria for admission of students. A charter school may accommodate the religious beliefs of its students and may by virtue of its design contain coreligionists. However, it cannot require that students be of a particular faith to attend.

A Religion Class That is Viewpoint Neutral Can be Taught in a Charter School

A religion course that is taught without advancing a religious viewpoint is constitutional. If the schools' board members, teachers, and students are primarily of the same faith, it is more likely that a religion course would be an unconstitutional endorsement of that religion. Religion courses must be viewpoint neutral. Cases that have examined religion courses look at the precise lessons and curriculum to see if they are an unconstitutional endorsement.

A Charter School Can Require a Course About Religion

A charter school may certainly offer courses about religion if the power to offer such a course is defined in its charter. Religion is a legitimate topic of study. The school would not have to allow students to opt-out of such a course if their parents found it offensive to their religious beliefs. Any religion course would have to avoid teaching that any religion is right or wrong and avoid endorsing any religious belief, religious belief generally, or nonbelief.

A Charter School Cannot Require Religious Exercises or Worship

A charter school cannot endorse or coerce prayer or religious worship. It cannot have Bible readings or prayers over the loudspeakers during the day or at assemblies. The school cannot authorize prayer in any situation. Prayer must be totally voluntary to students. A charter school cannot require religious exercises or worship. Students may initiate prayer so long as it does not materially disrupt the school.

A Charter School Cannot Identify With a Denomination

Whether a school can affiliate or identify with a denomination will be determined by the state's enabling statute. If the statute defines charter schools as state actors, they almost certainly cannot affiliate with a denomination because to do so would endorse that religion. If the statute is drawn so as to define charter schools as private actors, then it is unclear whether a charter can so affiliate; however, it would probably be unconstitutional because of the way charter schools are funded.

States Can Probably Exclude Religion-Based Charter Schools From Forming

States cannot discriminate against the religious viewpoint. However, the religious viewpoint is only protected when the right to Free Speech is protected. In all of the cases where the Supreme Court required that access be given to a religious group, that access was based on the right to freedom of speech within a limited public forum. The state cannot exclude the religious viewpoint from a limited public forum, though the state can exclude the subject of religion. States can probably deny charters to schools that seek to form with a religious character. It seems unlikely that states can deny charters to otherwise secular schools that are formed because of religious motivations.

WHAT RELIGION-BASED CHARTER SCHOOLS CAN AND CANNOT ACCOMPLISH

This study has attempted to answer the question whether religious charter schools can be constitutional. A better way to phrase this question is: What can religion-based charter schools accomplish? A religion based charter school cannot offer courses taught from a religious viewpoint, cannot maintain religious criteria for staff or for admission, cannot require religious exercises or worship, and cannot affiliate with a denomination. It is very likely that religious organizations cannot operate charter schools, though clergy can certainly sit on charter boards.

Whether a charter school can share facilities with a religious school would depend on their legal relationship and the specific factual situation. Charter schools may not endorse a belief system. Hence, they cannot have religious admission or employment criteria or offer a course from a religious viewpoint. Such actions would clearly endorse a particular belief.

On the other hand, charter schools can teach courses, even required ones, about religion and teach about the relationship between religion and morality, so long as those courses or lessons do not endorse religion. The fact that coreligionists share values does not prevent them from creating a character-based charter school. Moreover, morally-based general propositions of good can be taught at a charter school. Coreligionists can form charter schools.

Charters can accommodate their schedules around after-school religious studies and can even form to provide religious students with a free public, secular education. Charter schools can require that teachers promote the worldview stated in their missions, while on school grounds. Lastly, charter schools can offer students a room where they can voluntarily pray.

Charter schools may accommodate their students' beliefs. Hence, charter schools may form to accommodate the scheduling requirements of afternoon religious schools. Such is an accommodation to practice, not an endorsement to practice. Requiring that students attend religious classes after school would endorse such a practice, but creating a schedule that enables such a practice accommodates students' and parents' beliefs. Moreover, the problem of endorsement is why a charter school can offer students a room in which to pray, but cannot have teachers lead prayer or require worship. Enabling students to pray accommodates their existing belief, but operating a required or voluntary religious service in school endorses the beliefs of that service.

ARE RELIGIOUS CHARTER SCHOOLS A GOOD IDEA?

What if all Schools Were Charter Schools?

In some respects, charter statutes are inherently unfair when one compares their benefits and burdens with those of public and private schools. Public schools have the benefit of state funding and the burdens of state regulation and oversight. Private schools have the burden of self-funding, but the benefit of near complete autonomy. Charter schools have the benefit of total, or partial, state funding and the benefit of general autonomy, with the burden of only limited regulation. The autonomy of charter schools varies from state to state.

On the other hand, charter schools have a different burden than either public or private schools: they are accountable to the state in a very drastic way. If a charter school does not meets its performance goals it will be closed by the state (Herszenhorn, 2004). A public or private school may lose its accreditation if it has consistently poor test scores or refuses to follow a state curriculum, but only in very rare cases will it be closed by the state and cease to exist.

There is no reason why all schools could not be accountable to the state in the same way that charter schools are. The distinction between public and private schools would be based on the nature of the political entity operating the school, not the nature of its operating structure. Several European countries use this model of education (Glenn, 1989). The American notion of separation between church and state is, however, very different from the European notion of that relationship. Truly private schools could of course still operate with more freedom than charters, but the lure of state funding would be difficult to resist (Glenn, 2000).

Such an arrangement would probably benefit education and parental involvement. If this were the case, religion-based charter schools would pose much more difficult constitutional questions because of the nonfunding principle developed by the Supreme Court in the 1970s. Although the nonfunding principle has been limited, it has not been overruled. If all public schools were charter schools, however, the schools could still only accommodate parents' religious belief and not endorse such beliefs. While under current practice the state and private religious organizations form partnerships, the partnership organizations are always definitely either state actors or private actors.

The Nonfunding Principle

When the early Establishment Clause cases developed the nonfunding principle, that is, it was unconstitutional for states to provide certain monetary aid to private schools, the vast majority of private schools were parochial schools (*Lemon v. Kurtzman*, 1971). The numbers of parochial schools was an extremely important rationale behind the nonfunding principle. In the 1970s, then Justice William Rehnquist pointed out that because the state funds all public education, faith-based schools are a minor part of any aid program (*Meek v. Pettinger*, Rehnquist, J., dissenting, 1975).

In the 1980s, the Supreme Court applied Rehnquist's view to specific funding that goes to parents who send their children to both public and private schools. However, charter funding goes directly to schools, not to parents. Consequently, if all charter schools were religious, it is unclear whether the nonfunding principle would apply.

What if an Area had no Secular Charter School?

If all schools became charter schools, it is possible that an area, particularly a rural area, could have only religion-based charter schools. Lessons about how to cope with this problem can be learned from the Dutch: in the Netherlands, the state funds both public and private schools that meet enrollment and quality requirements (Glenn, 1989, p. 48). The "responsible authority" for each school can be a religious organization, a secular organization, or a governmental organization; in 1980, 70% of elementary students attended schools operated by nongovernmental institutions.

Dutch educational law promotes diversity by maintaining different standards for school closings on the basis of enrollment. A school in a community with a population of 250,000 will close if it cannot maintain an enrollment of more than 50 students for three years. However, if there is no school with that worldview within three kilometers, the enrollment requirement is only 30 students. Municipalities are also encouraged to provide transportation subsidies so students can attend a school of their worldview (Glenn, 1989, p. 48).

American courts would be unlikely to require districts to operate schools with a particular worldview because the courts have tried as much as possible to avoid telling administrators how to operate schools (*San Antonio v. Rodriguez*, 1973). On the other hand, an educational system that did not provide a religiously neutral option would undoubtedly be unconstitutional. School districts could of course take it upon themselves to operate a religiously neutral school in order to ensure that their school systems are constitutional. Moreover, school districts could offer transportation vouchers to schools that are religiously neutral. School districts could not use such a system to segregate students on the basis of race or religion.

CONCLUSIONS

Charter schools offer a tremendous opportunity for education in this country to reshape itself. The greatest shift is that they allow the transfer of some power and control from the state to parents. Parents will often know what is best for their children. Public education is one of the few instances in which the state becomes involved on a regular basis with making important "parental" decisions, rather than only becoming involved in extreme instances.

Religious parents are often the ones who are the most involved and interested in their children's education. Some parents feel religiously compelled to educate their children (*Murphy v. Arkansas*, 1988). Others are vigilant monitors, watching their children's lessons to make sure they are not being taught religiously objectionable material (*Mozert v. Hawkins*, 1987).

Since one of the goals of charter schools is to increase parental involvement, allowing religion-based charter schools is logical, though not necessarily good or bad. Once the state begins to tip the balance of power over to parents, religious parents ought to be included. Religion-based charter schools enable parents to form schools that respect and adapt to religious viewpoints without compromising the continuity of the school. Even if overtly religious schools are unconstitutional, charter schools can create an environment where students' religious beliefs are respected and protected for the sake of those beliefs.

Because state law defines charter schools, state legislators have tremendous power to change the way that they function. This book has generally assumed that charter schools are state actors and that state charter schemes will continue to operate more or less as they have. There are, however, two additional possibilities. States could rewrite their laws to make charters no longer state actors in order to exempt charter schools from various constitutional requirements.

If states do that, then all, or most, of the answers given by this study are called into question. State legislators could also begin to redefine charters and vouchers until they merged into a funding system that is neither one nor the other. If such a system included religious schools it would not be necessarily constitutional. Such a system would require an entirely new analysis.

Allowing denominational charter schools is unconstitutional. *Zelman v. Simmons-Harris* (2002), the recent Supreme Court voucher decision, does not provide an opening for denominational charters because charter schools are public schools, not private schools. The greatest potential that charter schools provides religious parents is that charter schools can accommodate religion and can be sensitive to religious students and parents in ways that public schools often are not.

Charter schools shift the balance of power in education away from the state and closer to parents. This shift does not allow parents to create any type of charter schools they'd like. Charter schools are still accountable to the state for educational results. One of the significant effects of this shift is that it allows parents to create public schools that accommodate their religious beliefs. The Constitution, however, prevents parents from creating charter schools that endorse their religious beliefs.

REFERENCES

Adam Abdulle Academy Web site. (2007). Retrieved January 18, 2007, from http://www.aaa.k12.mn.us/

Adler v. Duval County School Board, 206 F.3d 1070 (11th Cir. 2000).

Agostini v. Felton, 521 U.S. 203 (1997).

Aguilar v. Felton, 473 U.S. 402 (1985).

Altman v. Bedford School District, 45 F.Supp. 368 (S.D. NY 1999).

Arons, S. (1983). *Compelling belief: The culture of American schooling*. Amherst: University of Massachusetts Press.

Baggett v. Bullitt, 377 U.S. 360 (1964).

Bagley v. Raymond Sch. Dept., 728 A.2d 127 (Me. 1999).

Barron v. Mayor and City Council of Baltimore, 7 Pet. (32 U.S.) 243 (1833).

Becket fund for religious liberty. (2003). *States*. Retrieved February 7, 2007, from http://www.blaineamendments.org/states/states.html

Berger, R. (1997). Government by judiciary: The transformation of the Fourteenth Amendment. Indianapolis, IL: Liberty Fund.

Bethel School District No. 403 v. Fraser, 478 U.S. 675 (1986).

Bierlein, L. (1997). The charter school movement. In D. Ravitch & J. Viteritti (Eds.), New schools for a new century (pp. 37-60). New Haven, CT: Yale Press.

Bierwirth, J. (1997). *Redefine school boundaries.* Retrieved February 7, 2007, from www.nwrel.org/nwedu/spring_97/article6.html

Blumenfeld, S. (1981). *Is public education necessary?* Greenwich, CT: Devin-Adair.

Board of Ed. of Central Sch. Dist. No. 1 v. Allen, 392 U.S. 236 (1968).

Board of Ed. of Kiryas Joel Village Sch. Dist. v. Grumet, 512 U.S. 687 (1994).

Board of Ed. of Monroe-Woodbury Central School Dist. v. Wieder, 531 N.Y.S.2d 889, 527 N.E.2d 767 (1988).

Board of Ed. of Westside Community Schools v. Mergens, 496 U.S. 226 (1990).

Board of Regents v. Roth, 408 U.S. 564 (1972).

Bolick, C. (1998). *Transformation: The promise and politics of empowerment*. Oakland, CA: Institute for Contemporary Studies.

Boring v. Buncombe County Board of Education, 98 F.3d 1474 (4th 1996).

Bork, R. (1990). *The Tempting of America: The political seduction of the law*. New York: Simon & Schuster.

Bossetti, L. (1998). *Canada's charter schools: Initial report* (SAEE Research Series #3). Kelowna: Society for the Advancement of Excellence in Education.

Boyd v. Harding Academy of Memphis, Inc., 88 F.3d 410 (1996).

Bowen v. Kendrick, 487 U.S. 589 (1988).

Brentwood v. Tennessee Secondary School Athletic Assoc., 531 U.S. 288 (2001).

Brodsky, A. (1999, January 1). *Kiryas Joel lawyer to study relevance of charter schools. Forward*, 9.

Brown v. Board of Education of Topeka, 347 U.S. 483 (1954).

Buechler, M. (1996). Charter School Legislation: 12 Criteria. Retrieved January 4, 2004, from edreform.com/pubs/buechler (Excerpted from Charter Schools: Legislation and Results After Four Years, Policy Report. Jan. 1996).

Cantwell v. Connecticut, 310 U.S. 296 (1940).

Capitol Square Advisory Board v. Pinette, 515 U.S. 753 (1995).

Carter, S. (1993). *The culture of disbelief: How American law and politics trivialize religious devotion*. New York: Doubleday.

Center for Education Reform (2004). Charter school laws across the states: Ranking and scorecard 8th edition: Strong laws produce better results. http:// Retrieved (DATE?), from www.edreform.com/_upload/charter_school_laws.pdf

Center for Education Reform. (2006). *National charter school data: New school estimates 2006-2007*. Retrieved February 7, 2007, from http://www.edreform.com/_upload/CER_charter_numbers.pdf

Center for Education Reform. (2007). *Charter law*. Retrieved February 12, 2007, from http://www.edreform.com/index.cfm?fuseAction=cLaw

Chamberlin v. Dade County Bd. of Pub. Instruction, 377 U.S. 402 (1964).

Chandler v. James, 985 F.Supp. 1094 (M.D. Ala. 1997).

Chubb, J. & Moe, T. (1990). *Politics markets and America's schools*. Washington, DC: Brookings Inst.

Church of Lukumi Babalu Aye, Inc. v. City of Hialeah, 508 U.S. 520 (1993).

City of Boerne v. Flores, Archbishop of San Antonio, 521 U.S. 507 (1997).

Cline v. Catholic Diocese of Toledo, 206 F.3d 651 (2000).

Columbia Union College v. Clarke, 159 F.3d 151 (4th Cir. 1998).

Committee for Public Education and Religious Liberty v. Nyquist, 413 U.S. 756 (1973).

Committee for Public Education and Religious Liberty v. Regan, 444 U.S. 646 (1980).

Coons, J. (Jan. 22, 1989). Don't limit "choice" to public schools only. *Los Angeles Times*, Part V, p. 5.

Cooper, B., Fusarelli, L., & Randall, E. V. (2004). *Better policies better schools: Theories and applications*. Upper Saddle River, Upper Saddle River, NJ: Pearson.

Cord, R. (1982). *Separation of church and state: Historical fact and current fiction*. New York: Lambeth Press.

Corp. of Presiding Bishop of the Church of Jesus Christ of Latter-Day Saints v. Amos, 483 U.S. 327 (1987).

County of Allegheny v. ACLU, 492 U.S. 573 (1989).

Council of Org. and Others for Educ. About Parochaid v. Governor of Michigan, 566 N.W.2d 208 (Mich. 1997).

Cramp v. Board of Public Instruction of Orange County Florida, 368 U.S. 278 (1961).

Dale, A. (1997). *II charter school: The process. Center for education reform.* Retrieved January 4, 2004, from edreform.com/pubs/chartii.html

Daugherty v. Vanguard Charter Academy, 116 F.Supp. 2d 897 (S.D. Mich. 2000).

Dewey, J. (1900/1969). The school and society. Chicago: University of Chicago Press.

Doe v. Human, 725 F.Supp. 1503 (W.D. Ark. 1989).

Dwyer, J. (1998). *Religious schools v. children's rights.* Ithaca: Cornell University Press.

East Hartford Education Association v. Board of Education of The Town of East Hartford, 562 F.2d 838 (2nd Cir. 1977)

Eckert, P. (1989). *Jocks and burnouts.* New York: Teacher's College Press.

Edwards v. Aguillard, 482 U.S. 578 (1987).

E.E.O.C. v. Kamehameha Schools, 990 F.2d 458 (9th Cir. 1993)

Ehrenreich, B. (2001). Nickel and Dimed: On (Not) Getting By in America. New York: Metropolitan Books.

Employment Div., Dept. of Human Resources of Oregon v. Smith, 494 U.S. 872, reh'g denied, 496 U.S. 913 (1990).

Engel v. Vitale, 370 U.S. 421 (1962).

Epperson v. Arkansas, 393 U.S. 97 (1968).

Everson v. Board of Ed of Ewing Twp., 330 U.S. 1 (1947).

42 U.S.C. § 1983.

42 U.S.C. § 2000e.

42 U.S.C. § 2000e-1.

42 U.S.C. § 2000e-2.

Farrington v. Tokushige, 273 U.S. 284 (1927).

FCC v. Pacifica Foundation, 438 U.S. 726 (1978).

Feldman, S. (1997). *Please don't wish me a Merry Christmas: A critical history of the separation of church and state.* New York: New York University Press.

Finn, C. E., Jr., Manno, B. V., & Vanourek, G. (2000). *Charter schools in action.* Princeton, NJ: Princeton University Press.

Fisher v. Clackamas County School District 12, 13 Or. App. 56, 507 P.2d 839 (1973)

Fiske, E., & Ladd, H. (2000). *When schools compete.* Harrisonburg, VA: R. R. Donnelley and Sons.

First Amendment. (1791).

Finn, C., Jr., (Dec. 10, 2003). Why not religious charter schools? *Education Week.* Retrieved January 4, 2004, from http://www.edweek.org/ew/ew_printstory.cfm?slug=15finn.h23

Friedman, M. (1955). *The role of government in education.* In R. Solo (Ed.), *Economics and the public interest.* Chapel Hill, NJ: Rutgers University Press.

Frost v. Hawkins County Board of Education, 851 F.2d 822 (6th Cir. 1988).

Fusarelli, L. D. (2003). *The political dynamics of school choice.* New York: Palgrave Macmillan.

Gallup Poll. (2006). Retrieved January 18, 2007, from http://www .galluppoll.com/content/?ci=1690&pg=2

Glenn, C. L. (1988). *The myth of the common school.* Amherst, MA: University of Massachusetts Press.

Glenn, C. L. (1989). *Choice of schools in six nations.* Washington, DC: U.S. Dept. of Education.

Glenn, C. L. (1998, Nov. 27). Justice Demands that parents have a choice. *Boston Globe (*Editorial), A31.

Glenn, C. L. (2000). *The ambiguous embrace.* New Jersey: Princeton University Press.

Goldman v. Weinberger, 475 U.S. 503 (1986).

Good News Club v. Milford Central School, 533 U.S. 98 (2001).

Goodstein, L. (Sept. 10, 1998). Fresh debate on 1802 Jefferson Letter. *New York Times,* p. A20.

Goldstein, J. (1998). Exploring "unchartered" territory: An analysis of charter schools and the applicability of the U.S. Constitution. *California Interdisciplinary Law Journal, 7,* 133–179.

Graff, G. (1992). *Beyond the culture wars.* New York: Norton.

Griffin v. County Sch. Bd of Prince Edward County, 377 U.S. 218 (1964).

Haft, W. (1998). Charter schools and the nineteenth century corporation: A Match made in the public interest. *Arizona State Law Journal, 30,* 1023.

Hall v. Board of School Commissioners of Conecuh County, 656 F.2d 999 (1981).

Harris Interactive Inc. (2003). While most Americans believe in God, only 36% Attend a religious service once a month or more often. Retrieved January 18, 2007, from http://www.harrisinteractive.com/harris_poll/index.asp?PID=408

Hartocollis, A. (1999, Feb. 1). A church's seeds for a charter school. *New York Times,* p. 33.

Hassel, B. (1998). Charter schools: Politics and practice. In P. Peterson & B. Hassel (Eds.), *Learning from school choice* (pp. 249-71). Washington, DC: Brookings Institute Press.

Hassel, B. (1999). *The charter school challenge: Avoiding the pitfalls, fulfilling the promise.* Harrisonburg, VA: R. R. Donnelley and Sons.

Hazelwood Sch. Dist. v. Kuhlmeier, 484 U.S. 260 (1988).

Henig, J. (1994). *Rethinking school choice.* New Jersey: Princeton University Press.

Hearne v. Illinois State Board of Educ., 706 N.E.2d 886 (IL 1999).

Herndon v. Chapel-Hill, 89 F.3d 174 (4th Cir. 1996).

Herszenhorn, D. M. (2004, Jan. 13). Report faults charter schools in New York. *New York Times,* p. A1.

Hill, P., Pierce, L., & Guthrie, J. (1997). *Reinventing public education.* Chicago: University of Chicago Press.

Hobbie v. Unemployment Appeals Comm'n of Fla., 480 U.S. 136 (1987).

Huffman, K. (1998). Charter schools, equal protection litigation, and the New School Reform Movement. *New York University Law Review, 73,* 1290-1327.

Hunter, J. (1991). *Culture wars.* New York: Basic Books.

Jackson v. Benson, 578 N.W.2d 602 (Wis. 1998), cert. denied, 525 U.S. 997 (1998).

Johnston, R. (September 8, 1999). Bush Zeroes In on Accountability For Federal K-12 Funds. *Education Week, 19*(1), 28.

Jorgenson, L. (1987). *The state and the non-public school.* Columbia: University of Missouri Press.

Kane, P. R. (1998). *New Jersey charter schools: the first year 1997-1998.* New York: Teachers College.

Kilpatrick, W. (1992). *Why Johnny can't tell right from wrong.* New York: Simon & Schuster.

Kolderie, T. (1993). *The states begin to withdraw the exclusive. In Public Services Redesign Project.* St. Paul, MN: Center for Policy Studies.

Lacks v. Ferguson Reorganized School District R-2, 147 F.3d 718 (8th Cir. 1998).

Lamb's Chapel v. Center Moriches Union Free Sch. Dist., 508 U.S. 384 (1993).

Lane, B. (1999). *Choice matters: Policy alternatives and implications for charter schools.* Retrieved February 7, 2007, from www.nwrel.org/charter/policy.html

Larkin v. Grendel's Den, Inc., 459 U.S. 116 (1982)

Larson, E. (1989). *Trial and error.* Oxford, England: Oxford University Press.

Lemon v. Kurtzman, 403 U.S. 602 (1971).

Lee v. Weisman, 505 U.S. 577 (1992).

Levy, L. (1994). *The Establishment Clause: Religion and the First Amendment.* Chapel Hill, NC: University of North Carolina Press.

Locke v. Davey, 540 U.S. 712 (2004).

Loewen, J. W. (1995). *Lies my teacher told me.* New York: The New Press.

Lynch v. Donnelly, 465 U.S. 668 (1984).

Mann, H. (1846). Tenth annual report of the Secretary of the Board of Education. In D. Davis (Ed.), *Antebellum American culture (pp. 40-43).* Lexington, MA: D.C. Heath & Co.

Marbury v. Madison, 5 U.S. 137 (1803).

Marsh v. Chambers, 463 U.S. 783 (1983).

McCaleb, I. C. (2001, Dec. 14). Bush education bill one step closer to law. *CNN.* Retrieved February 7, 2007, from http://www.cnn.com/2001/ALLPOLITICS/12/13/house.education/index.html

McCollum v. Board of Ed. Dist. No. 71 Champaign City, 333 U.S. 203 (1948).

McCreary County, Ky. v. American Civil Liberties Union of Ky., 545 U.S. 844 (2005).

McDaniel v. Paty, 435 U.S. 618 (1978).

McGowan v. Maryland, 366 U.S. 420 (1961).

Medeiros v. Kiyosaki, 52 Haw. 436, 478 P.2d 314 (HI. 1970).

Medler, A. (1996). Promise and progress. *American School Board Journal, 183*(3), 26-28.

Meek v. Pettinger, 421 U.S. 349, reh'g denied, 422 U.S. 1049 (1975).

Melzer v. Board of Education of the City School District of the City of New York, 336 F.3d 185 (2nd Cir. 2003)

Meyer v. Nebraska, 262 U.S. 390 (1923).

Mich. Comp. Laws Ann. § 380.501. (2004)

Mich. Comp. Laws Ann. § 380.502.

Minn. Stat. Ann. §120.064. (West 1993 & Supp. 1997).

Minn. Stat. Ann. § 124D.10 subd. 8 (2004).

Miles v. Denver Public Schools, 944 F.2d 773 (10th Cir. 1991).

Mitchell v. Helms, 530 U.S. 793 (2000).

Monsma, S. (1993). *Positive neutrality.* Grand Rapids MI: Baker Books.

Morken, H., & Formicola, J. (1999). *The politics of school choice.* Lanham, MD: Rowman & Littlefield.

Morton, v. Board of Education of the City of Chicago, 69 Ill.App.2d 38, 216 N.E.2d 305 (IL 1966).

Mozert v. Hawkins County Board of Education, 827 F.2d 1058 (6th Cir. 1987).

Mt. Healthy City Sch. Dist. Bd. of Ed. v. Doyle, 429 U.S. 274 (1977).

Mueller v. Allen, 463 U.S. 388 (1983).

Murdock v. Pennsylvania, 319 U.S. 105 (1943).

Murphy v. Arkansas, 852 F.2d 1039 (8th Cir. 1988).

N.Y. Educ. Law § 414. (McKinney 2000).

N.Y. Educ. Law § 2854. (McKinney 2000).

National Commission an Excellence in Education (1984/1994). *A Nation at Risk.* Portland, OR: USA Research.

National Gay Task Force v. Board of Education of the City of Oklahoma City, 729 F.2d 1270 (10th Cir. 1984).

Nylen, C. (1990, April). *Character education: An elementary teacher's view, in better school, better lives: An invitation to dialogue.* Boston: Boston University Center for Advancement of Ethics and Character.

Parachoid v. Governor of Michigan, 548 N.W.2d 909 (Mich. Ct. App. 1996).

Peloza v. Capistrano, 37 F.3d 517 (9th Cir. 1994).

Perry Education Assoc. v. Perry Local Educators' Assoc., 460 U.S. 37 (1983).

Perry v. Milwaukee Public Schools, 12 Fed.Appx. 406 (7th Cir. 2001).

Perry v. Sindermann, 408 U.S. 593 (1972).

Peterson, P. (1990). Monoploy and competition in American education. In W. Clune & J. Witte (Eds.), *Choice and control in American education* (Vol. 1). London: Falmer Press

Pfeffer, L. (1967). *Church state and freedom.* Boston: Beacon Press.

Pickering v. Board of Education of Township High School District 205, 391 U.S. 563 (1968).

Pierce v. Society of Sisters of the Holy Name of Jesus and Mary, 268 U.S. 510 (1925).

Plyler v. Doe, 457 U.S. 202, reh'g denied, 458 U.S. 1131 (1982).

Powell, A. (1985). *The shopping mall high school.* Boston: Houghton Mifflin.

Profiles of Minnesota Charter Schools. (2007). Retrieved January 18, 2007, from http://www.centerforschoolchange.org/

Quality counts '98: The urban challenge (1998, January 8). *Education Week, 17,* 12.

Ravitch, D. (1974). *Great school wars.* New. York, Basic Books

Research issue of the week: Charter schools. (1998, Sep. 7). *Policy.com.* Retrieved January 4, 2004, from www.policy.com/issuewk/98/0907/090798.html

Reynolds v. U.S., 98 U.S. 145 (1878).

Roberts v. Madigan, 921 F.2d 1047 (10th Cir. 1990)

Rosenberger v. Rector and Visitors of the University of Virginia, 515 U.S. 819 (1995).

Rendell-Baker v. Kohn, 457 U.S. 830 (1982)

Reutter, E., Jr. (1994). *Law of Public Education* (4th ed.). Westbury, NY: Foundation Press.

Roemer v. Board of Pubic Works of Maryland, 426 U.S. 736 (1976).

Rosenberger Brigham Assoc. (1998). *Innovation & Massachusetts charter schools* (for the Massachusetts Department of Education). Retrieved January 4, 2004, from www.doe.mass.edu/cs.www/imcs98/798Report.html

Rotherham, A. (1999, Feb. 24). When it comes to school size, smaller is better. *Education Week, 18*(24), 76

San Antonio Indep. Sch. Dist. v. Rodriguez, 411 U.S. 1 (1973).

Santa Fe Independent School District v. Doe, 530 U.S. 290 (2000).

Sarason, S. (1998). *Charter schools: Another flawed educational reform?* New York: Teacher's College.

School Dist. of Abington Twp. v. Schempp, 374 U.S. 203 (1963).

School Dist. of the City of Grand Rapids v. Ball, 473 U.S. 373 (1985).

Sciolino, E. (2004, February 11). Debate begins in France on religion in the schools. *New York Times.* Retrieved June 3, 2007, from http://select.nytimes.com/search/restricted/article?res=F20613FA3e5F0C778CDDAB0894DC404482

Simmon-Harris v. Goff, 86 Ohio St.3d 1, 711N.E.2d 203 (1999).

Simmons-Harris v. Zelman, 234 F.3d 945 (6th Cir. 2000).

Sizer, T. (1992). *Horace compromize: The dilemma of the American high school.* USA: Houghton Mifflin.

Sloan v. Lemon, 413 U.S. 825 (1973).

Smith v. Board of School Commissioners of Mobile County, 827 F.2d 684 (11th Cir. 1987).

Somerville, S. (Spring 2001). Legalizing Home Schooling in America. *Private School Monitor, 21*(4), 1-11.

South Dakota v. Dole, 483 U.S. 203 (1987).

Stark v. Independent School Dist., No. 640, 123 F.3d 1068 (8th Cir. 1997).

State of Nebraska ex rel. The School District Of Hartington v. Nebraska State Board of Education, 188 Neb. 1, 195 N.W.2d 161 (1972).

Stone v. Graham, 449 U.S. 39 (1980).

Swanson By and Through Swanson v. Guthrie Independent School Dist. No. I-L, 135 F.3d 694 (10th Cir. 1998).

Sweet, L. (1997). *God in the classroom.* Toronto, Canada: McClelland & Stewart.

Texas Monthly, Inc. v. Bullock, 489 U.S. 1 (1989).

Thiessen, E. J. (1993). *Teaching for commitment: Liberal education, indoctrination & Christian nature.* United Kingdom: McGill-Queens University Press.

Tilton v. Richardson, 403 U.S. 672 reh'g denied 404 U.S. 874 (1971).

Tinder, G. (1989, Dec.). Can we be good without God? *Atlantic Monthly,* p. 69.

Torcaso v. Watkins, 367 U.S. 488 (1961).

Tribe, L. (1985). *Constitutional choices.* Cambridge, MA: Harvard University Press.

Trop v. Dulles, 356 U.S. 86 (1958).

Turekian, K. (1997). Traversing the minefields of educational reform: The legality of charter Schools. *Connecticut Law Review, 29,* 1365.

Van Orden v. Perry, 545 U.S. 677, (2005).

Viteritti, J. (1999). *Choosing equality: School choice, the Constitution, and civil society.* Washington, DC: Brookings.

Ward v. Hickey, 996 F.2d 448 (1st Cir. 1993).

Washegesic v. Bloomingdale, 813 F.Supp. 559 (WD Mich. 1993).

Wallace v. Jaffree, 472 U.S. 38 (1985).

Walsh M. (1999, July 14). Critics See Fatal Legal Flaws In Vote on Commandments. *Education Week, 18*(42), 24.

Walz v. Tax Com. of the City of New York, 397 U.S. 664 (1970).

Weaver v. Nebo School District, 1998 WL 912110 (D.Utah 1998).

Weeres, J. (1990). Is more or less choice needed? In W. Boyd (Ed.), *Choice in education: Potential and problems.* Berkeley, CA: McCutchan.

Weinberg, L., Russo, C., & Osborne, A. (1998). The Establishment Clause, Agostini v. Felton, and vouchers in religiously affiliated non-public schools. *International Journal of Educational Reform, 7,* 209–216.

West Virginia v. Barnette, 319 U.S. 624 (1943).

Widmar v. Vincent, 454 U.S. 263 (1981).

Wieman v. Updegraff, 344 U.S. 183 (1952).

Wiley v. Franklin, 468 F.Supp. 133 (E.D. Tenn. 1979).

Wiley v. Franklin, 497 F.Supp. 390 (E.D. Tenn. 1980).

Willis, G. (1990). *Under God: Religion and American politics.* New York: Simon & Schuster.

Wis. Stat. Ann. § 119.23 (West, 1999).

Wisconsin v. Yoder, 406 U.S. 205 (1972).

Wise, A. (1968). *Rich schools, poor schools.* Chicago: University of Chicago Press.

Witters v. Washington Dept. of Serv. for the Blind, 474 U.S. 481 (1986).

Wolman v. Walter, 433 U.S. 229 (1977).

Woodward, B., & Armstrong, A. (1979). *The brethren: Inside the Supreme Court.* New York: Simon & Schuster

Wynne, E., & Ryan, K. (1997). Reclaiming our schools: Teaching character, academics, and discipline (2nd ed.). Boston: Prentice-Hall.

Zellers v. Huff, 55 N.M. 501, 236 P.2d 949 (1951).

Zelman v. Simmons-Harris, 536 U.S. 639 (2002).

Zobrest v. Catalina Foothills Sch. Dist., 509 U.S. 1 (1993).

Zorach v. Clauson, 343 U.S. 306 (1952).

Printed in the United States
215289BV00002B/1/A